1. HIROSHIGE, A Waterfall

No one explored the technical processes of colored woodblock printing more impressively than this artist. Here the falling water, the clouds and the rock have almost lost all reality, yet they dazzle us with their poetic values.

13⁷⁄₁₆″ x 9¹⁄₁₆″, from the author's collection.

A TREASURY

OF THE WORLD'S

GREAT PRINTS

A collection of the best-known woodcuts,
etchings, engravings and lithographs
by twenty-three great artists,
selected and presented by

Stephen Longstreet

SIMON AND SCHUSTER

NEW YORK

LIBRARY OF CONGRESS CATALOG CARD NUMBER: 61–12867
MANUFACTURED IN THE UNITED STATES OF AMERICA

ACKNOWLEDGMENTS

OF THE MANY MUSEUMS, libraries and public collections that have let me freely roam their print and drawing rooms and probe their manuscripts and documents over the last twenty years, I want to thank in particular the Bibliothèque Nationale, the Sorbonne, the Musée du Louvre, the Library of the Institut de France and the Institut de Géographie et d'Économie, all of Paris; the Nationalgalerie and the Kaiser Friedrich Museum, Berlin; the Cabinet des Estampes, Brussels; the Ryksmuseum, Amsterdam; the Vatican Library and the Biblioteca Hertzuana, both of Rome, and the Museo Nazionale, Naples; the Prado, Madrid; the Albertina Museum, Vienna; the British Museum, the Royal Collection at Windsor Castle, the Victoria and Albert Museum, all in London, the Ashmolean Museum at Oxford and the Devonshire Collection at Chatsworth. And I shall always be grateful to the late Bernard Berenson for giving me the run of his magnificent library at I Tatti.

In America I owe much to the Fogg Museum; to the Library of Congress, the Freer Gallery, the National Gallery of Art and the Phillips Memorial Gallery, all of Washington, D. C.; to the Pierpont Morgan Library, the Metropolitan Museum of Art, the Museum of Modern Art, Cooper Union Museum and the New York Public Library, all of New York City; to the Boston Institute of Fine Arts; and to the Huntington Library in California.

The Japanese sections are the result of several prolonged journeys to that country. I thank the Tokyo National Museum and the Nezu and Nagoo museums, also in Tokyo; the Koryu-ji Museum at Kyoto; and the Hokke-ji Nunnery and the Bunkakan Collection, both at Nara. Among experts and collectors I thank that fine historian of art, the late Yukio Yashiro, and those collectors whose names are listed in my notebooks as J. Kosaka, Ogunra, L. Hikone, K. Hara, Magoshi, Maisunaga and Sorimachi.

I have also received valuable help from Lorser Feitelson and Helen Lundeberg, painters and collectors; Helen Wurdemann, director of a true haven for art in southern California, the Los Angeles Art Association; Justin Thannhauser, friend and collector of the moderns; Stanton Macdonald-Wright, who turned to the East with rewarding results; the late Judson D. Metzgar, who knew more than most about Japanese prints; Lilla Perry, who opened her remarkable collections to us; George Longstreet, expert and world's largest collector of Daumier prints; Ebria Feinblatt, curator of prints and drawings, Los Angeles County Museum; Jake Zeitlin and O. P. Reed, rare book and print collectors; Lessing J. Rosenwald, who came to our studio to talk of prints and offered freely the inspection of his Jenkintown collections, and Felix Guggenheim, for many kindnesses; the print hunters, many of them old friends: Marcel LeComte and Paul Proute of Paris, Walter Schatzki and William Lee Comerford of New York City, Robert Maroni and Robert Light of Boston, and Harry Nail of Palo Alto; and Edwin Grabhorn of San Francisco, a great collector.

Of men now dead whose collections have since been dispersed, I remember with pleasure consulting Louis V. Ledoux, Arthur Davis Ficke, Walter Arensburg (we disagreed only on the Bacon-Shakespeare hassle) and Frank Lloyd Wright.

The actual prints reproduced in this book are from the following collections: Metropolitan Museum of Art, Museum of Modern Art, National Gallery of Art, Brooklyn Museum. The Daumier prints are from the George Longstreet and Helen Wurdemann collections. The Japanese prints and those by Winslow Homer are from the author's collection.

There is one more group to thank—those earnest, hard-working people on the publisher's staff who did the legwork in compiling the reproductions and who designed the book: first of all, an old friend of long standing in whose office the project first came to life, my editor, Henry W. Simon; and Elizabeth Sutherland, Helen Barrow and Frank Metz, who gave me much aid.

This listing of acknowledgments could be twice as long, but I hope that memory and notes have recorded the major contributors.

Stephen Longstreet

Palazzo Gritti, Venice
Elm Drive, California

CONTENTS

		PAGE
1. HIROSHIGE, A Waterfall		*Frontispiece*
Acknowledgments		5
A Word Before the Pictures		15
The Prints and Their Makers		21

ALBRECHT DÜRER *German School 1471-1528*   23

    2. The Adoration of the Magi   22
    3. Erasmus of Rotterdam   25
    4. The Knight, Death and the Devil   27
    5. Adam and Eve   28
    6. Melancholia I   29
    7. The Great Horse   30
    8. The Apocalypse: Saint Michael and His Angels   31
    9. The Riders on the Four Horses   32
    10. Rhinoceros   33
    11. The Cannon   34

PIETER BRUEGHEL *Flemish 1525(?)-1569*   35

    12. Summer   36
    13. Penitent Magdalen   38
    14. Psyche with Mercury   39
    15. Seven Deadly Sins: Pride   40
    16. Seven Virtues: Temperance   41
    17. Seven Virtues: Faith   42
    18. Seven Deadly Sins: Envy   43
    19. Seven Deadly Sins: Sloth   44
    20. Seven Virtues: Prudence   45
    21. Seven Virtues: Justice   46
    22. Seven Deadly Sins: Lust   47
    23. Luilekkerland, or The Land of Cockayne   48

JACQUES CALLOT *French 1592-1635*   49

    24. Pantaloon   50
    25. Temptation of St. Anthony   53

26–31. Miseries of War   54–56

32. The Bohemians   57

33. The Bohemians   57

34. View of Pont Neuf   58

35. The Great Fair at Impruneta   58

REMBRANDT HARMENSZ VAN RIJN *Dutch* 1606-1669   59

36. Rembrandt Leaning on a Stone Sill   61

37. Descent from the Cross by Torchlight   62

38. Christ with the Sick Around Him, Receiving Little Children (The "Hundred Guilder" Print)   63

39. Woman Sitting Beside a Stove   64

40. The Goldweigher's Field   66–67

41. Landscape with Hay Barn and Flock of Sheep   69

42. View of Amsterdam   69

43. Great Jewish Bride   70

44. Great Jewish Bride   71

45. The Large Lion Hunt   72

46. Faust in His Study Watching a Magic Disc   73

47. Landscape with Cottage and a Large Tree   74–75

48. Landscape with Trees, Farm Buildings and a Tower   74–75

49. Thomas J. Haaring ("The Young Haaring")   76

WILLIAM HOGARTH *English* 1697-1764   77

50. The Harlot's Progress: Arrival in London   81

51. The Harlot's Progress: Her Funeral   82

52. The Rake's Progress: He Entertains   83

53. The Rake's Progress: In Bedlam   84

54. Strolling Actresses: Dressing in a Barn   87

55. Marriage à la Mode: Breakfast Scene   88

56. Marriage à la Mode: The Quack Doctor   89

57. Election: Canvassing for Votes   90

58. Election: Voting   91

59. Election: An Election Entertainment   94

60. A Company of Undertakers or A Consultation of Physicians   95

GIOVANNI BATTISTA PIRANESI *Italian* 1720-1778   96

61–66. Prisons   97–103

FRANCISCO JOSÉ DE GOYA Y LUCIENTES *Spanish* 1746-1828   104

67. Self-portrait   105

68–74. Caprichos   107–115

75. Pedro Romeno   117

76. Spanish Pastime   118

77. Brave Bull   119

78. Divided Arena   120

79. The Proverbs   121

CONTENTS

80–83. Disasters of War 122–125
    84. Caprichos 126

THOMAS ROWLANDSON *English 1756-1827*   127
    85. The Sculptor Nollekens and His Venus 129
    86. Careless Attention 130
    87. Grog on Board 130
    88. Miseries of Social Life 131
    89. Miseries of Human Life, Title Page 132
    90. Painter Disturbed 134
    91. Miseries, Domestic 137
    92. Miseries of Social Life 137
    93. Sports of a Country Fair 138
    94. The Last Jig! 139
    95. Amputation 140

JAMES GILLRAY *English 1757-1815*   141
    96. The Morning After Marriage 142
    97. A Voluptuary 143
    98. A Cognoscente 144
    99. The Cow Pock 147
    100. The Pic-Nic Orchestra 148
    101. The Gout 149
    102. Dido Forsaken 150
    103. A March to the Bank 151
    104. Frying Sprats 152
    105. Toasting Muffins 153

WILLIAM BLAKE *English 1757-1827*   154
    106. Book of Job: When the Morning Stars Sang Together 155
    107. Book of Job: Behemoth and Leviathan 156
    108. Book of Job: There Were Not Found Women Fair as the
         Daughters of Job 157
    109. Dante's Inferno: The Malebranche Tormenting Ciampolo 159
    110. Dante's Inferno: The Whirlwind of Lovers 160
    111. Dante's Inferno: The Circle of the Falsifiers 161
    112. Jerusalem: ". . . Leaning against the pillars." 162
    113. America: Frontispiece 163

KATSUSHIKA HOKUSAI *Japanese 1760-1849*   165
    114. A Folk Hero 166
    115. A Battle 167
    116. A Duel 168
    117. Farm Life 170
    118. Crossing Stream 171
    119. Scene from a Legend 173
    120. The 47 Ronin 174
    121. On the Tokaido Road 175

CONTENTS

122. A Moon Bridge   176–177
123. Lake View   178

TOSHUSAI SHARAKU *Japanese* active circa 1794   181

124. Actor in Female Part   179
125. Actor Playing a Money Lender   180
126. Actor as a Young Girl   189
127. Actor Playing a Fish Peddler   190
128. The Actor-Manager   191

UTAGAWA HIROSHIGE *Japanese* 1797-1858   198

129. Snow Scene   192–193
130. Fireworks at Night   194
131. Bird over Landscape   195
132. Mountain Landscape   196

HONORÉ DAUMIER *French* 1808-1879   200

133. In the Box   202
134. Set Him Free, He Is No Longer Dangerous   203
135. The Accused Can Now Have His Say   204
136. P-s-s-t!   207
137. Music at Home   208
138. Café Politics   209
139. The Happy Audience   210
140. Discussion in the Gallery   211
141. The Empire Is at Peace   213
142. End of the Second Empire   214

JAMES ABBOTT McNEILL WHISTLER *American* 1834-1903   216

143. Thames Set: Limehouse   217
144. Thames Set: Rotherhithe   218
145. Thames Set: Hungerford   220
146. Thames Set: Longshoreman   221
147. Thames Set: Eagle Wharf   222
148. Thames Set: Westminster Bridge   223
149. Venice Set: Bridge   224
150. Venice Set: Nocturne   225
151. Venice Set: Doorway   226

WINSLOW HOMER *American* 1836-1910   227

152. Sharpshooter   228
153. Thanksgiving in Camp   229
154. A Parisian Ball   230
155. Dancing at the Mabille, Paris   231
156. Winter   232
157. On the Beach   233
158. Waiting   234
159. Gloucester Harbor   235

CONTENTS

160. On the Bluff 236

161. Gloucester Harbor   237

PAUL GAUGUIN *French 1848-1903*   238

162. Offerings. 239

163. The Gods (Te Atua)   240

164. Night Eternal (Te Po)   241

165. The Locusts and the Ants   243

166. Title Page for "The Smile"   244

167. Wonderful Earth (Nave Nave Fenua)   245

168. Woman at the River (Auti te Pape)   246–247

169. Fragrance (Noa Noa)   248

EDVARD MUNCH *Norwegian 1863-1944*   249

170. The Death Chamber   251

171. The Young Model   252

172. Anxiety   254

173. The Shriek   255

174. The Kiss   256

175. Two Beings   257

176. Tête-à-Tête   259

177. Omega's Eyes   261

178. Jealousy   262

179. Violin Concert   263

HENRI DE TOULOUSE-LAUTREC *French 1864-1901*   264

180. Woman Preparing Bathtub   265

181. Woman in Bed   265

182. Mlle. Marcelle Lender   266

183. Divan Japonais   267

184. Clown at the Moulin Rouge (Cha-U-Ka-O)   268

185. The Costume Ball at the Moulin Rouge   270

186. Woman in a Corset   272

187. At the Moulin Rouge: La Goulue and Her Sister   273

188. Yvette Guilbert   274

189. The Jockey   275

HENRI MATISSE *French 1869-1954*   277

190. Crouching Nude with Black Hair   278

191. Nude Study   279

192. Girl with a Vase of Flowers   281

193. Nude   283

194. Arabesque   284

195. Odalisque in a Tulle Skirt   285

196. The Blinding of Polyphemus   286

197. Nude, Arms Clasped over Head   287

198. Charles Baudelaire   288

199. Drawing from *Anthology of the Amours of Ronsard*   289

CONTENTS

CONTENTS

GEORGES ROUAULT *French* 1871-1958   290

200. Know ye that so many of us as were baptized into Jesus
     Christ were baptized into His death   292
201. The society lady fancies she has a reserved seat in heaven   294
202. We think ourselves kings   295
203. Love ye one another   296
204. The law is hard, but it is the law   297
205. Sometimes the blind have comforted those who can see   298
206. Obedient unto death, even the death of the cross   299
207. My sweet homeland, what has become of you?   301
208. War, which all mothers hate   302
209. This will be the last time, little father!   303
210. Arise, ye dead!   304
211. The Prostitute   305
212. Flotsam   306
213. Self-portrait   307
214. Portrait of a Man   308

PABLO PICASSO *Spanish* 1881-   309

215. The Frugal Repast   310
216. Mother Combing Her Hair   312
217. Still Life with Bottle   313
218. Sculptor and Model   314
219. Minotauromachy   315
220. Weeping Woman   317
221. The Cock   318
222. Young Boy   320
223. Toad   321
224. The Seated Woman, after Cranach the Younger   323

MARC CHAGALL *Russian* 1887-   324

225. Cover for La Fontaine's *Fables*   326
226. La Fontaine's *Fables:* Cat Changed to a Woman   327
227. La Fontaine's *Fables:* The Swan and the Cook   328
228. La Fontaine's *Fables:* The Lion and the Hunter   329
229. Jacob Blessing the Children of Joseph   330
230. The Bible: Jacob's Dream   331
231. The Bible: Solomon Proclaimed King   332
232. The Rainbow   333

A Word Before the Pictures

THE IDEA of this book is very simple: to present pictures for you to look at, pictures that are not oil paintings or water colors or Chinese ink scrolls, but prints—pictures made to be printed from plates of wood, metal or stone.

It is not primarily a book about the techniques of print making, though some of these will be explained. It is for the pleasure of seeing and absorbing some of the world's great prints, in each of which the artist, like some film director of genius, is the graphic historian of his society. Looking at them, our eyes change the inky lines into images of what we once were like, why and how we lived and loved and politicked and dressed and acted.

Just as we do not ask of a great motion picture that it intrude on us with details of lens changes, cutting or dubbing, so in these pages we will not dwell on the technical details of how the artists made their prints. Instead the text is about the artists themselves, and about their times. The words are meant to be merely a kind of mood music, to try to suggest what life felt like when these prints were made, how things tasted, the way artists looked at the world, and what angers, loves and pleasures they had in the vision of mankind they put down for us.

The surprising thing is how like us they were—in their fear of war, of disasters, and in their concern, both in high and in low places, for the wretched lot of so much of mankind. And how often their ideas of fun seem like ours. As we study some of their strong, realistic images of wilder and cruder times, they begin to relate to our own laments and joys in the baffling society of today.

The artist is not some dilettante in a nylon tower, locked away from the world. He is like the average citizen, but with keen powers of observation which are given to few of us, with a deeper feeling for and a closer understanding of humanity. Like us he is touched by beauty, hurt by meanness, shocked at evil. He projects for us those things we sense but are not able ourselves to put down in any permanent form.

One can look at some of these pictures and catch their meaning

and their story at first glance. But not every print steps forward to expose its face or landscape at once; some one must read bit by bit, like a letter or a favorite book, savoring each small detail that goes to make up the greater whole. These are pictures to look at often—then they will reveal themselves gladly and be seen as the artists meant them to be seen.

It is not for any particular message, any special philosophy that this book has been put together, but only for the pleasure of looking.

HOW IT BEGAN

WHEN primitive man had fed himself and seen to the fire, he had the leisure to lie back and see faces in the clouds, and also the shapes of the animals he hunted—or which hunted him. He began to see some likenesses of familiar objects in the bark of tree trunks, the cracks of rock formations, and he must have started scratching marks on such surfaces himself, delighting over his crude creations. Soon his drawings of animals and of his own rituals, and his use of picture-making as tribal magic, were an established part of his life. These pictures became art, even if the critic, the dealer and the museum expert were thousands of years away. The making of symbols with line and form and color was there from the beginning.

It took a long time before anyone could think of a method by which an art image could be reproduced, a way actual copies could be made of the originals. The first prints were simple stone or wood rubbings. They were made by pressing a paperlike sheet of material against some stone or wood form carved in low relief and rubbing the back of the paper with soot or charcoal. The deep-carved lines would come out white and a kind of negative of the picture would appear. Children still use this method to make prints of heads on coins, rubbing a pencil over the back of a bit of paper pressed against the metal disk.

But this was not creative print making, and in time the actual method of taking a print was developed: the making of impressions from wooden or metal forms on which a picture had been engraved or cut by a tool.

The dating of the early making of prints, after first guesses, has been driven back further and further into history. It was once accepted that the earliest were the first Gothic prints dating from around the

fifteenth century, but the archaeologist Sir Aurel Stein found in the Caves of a Thousand Buddhas, on the western border of China, woodcut prints of Buddhist images that could be dated 868 A.D. Prints found in Tunhwang are dated 947 and 983. The actual discovery of print making must have been even earlier. There were at this time also experiments in color printing of an image of Avalokitesvara. During the T'ang period (618-907) textiles were printed from color blocks. Much later—in the early seventeenth century—books of Chinese color prints were being printed as regular items of trade. Soon some very remarkable prints appeared in books on the art of drawing. The most famous of these is *The Mustard Seed Garden (Chien Tzu Yuan)*.

The Japanese woodcut prints of the seventeenth century, called *ukiyoye*, do not owe as much to Chinese art as some think. There was a cultural influence, but while the Chinese prints are usually copies of existing works of art, the great Japanese woodcut artists—men like Moronobu, Kiyomasu, Sharaku, Utamaro—were usually original creators of the subjects in their prints. The Chinese printed on a thin white paper that took color well, but the Japanese used a tougher, softer paper made from the bark of the mulberry tree and got a more delicate color balance and depth of tone as the colors sank into the paper, so the design could be seen from the back of the print. The best of these Japanese prints, mere folk art in their time, are among the great art treasures of the world.

In the Western world it is not until the fifteenth century that we hear of a woodcutters' guild (of professional print makers), and in northern Europe the cutter, or *Formenschneider*, worked independently of the artist. The *Heiligenbilder*, or saints' prints, were all of a religious nature, the production centers for them being those cities along trade routes or near holy shrines where travelers and pilgrims could buy impressions from wood or metal cuts to take home in memory of their trip. They were mostly hand-colored and often very crude. The merit of such prints is historical rather than artistic, but collectors, the natural prey of dealers, pay fabulous prices for them because of their rarity. Most of this work of the fifteenth century is anonymous; sometimes the initials of the cutter are given. The creators of the first prints are identified by such names as "the Master of the Banderoles," "the Master of the Region of Cologne," "Master E. S.," "Master W. with the Key."

By the middle of the century there are well-known masters of the print: Schongauer, van Meckenem, Pollaiuolo, Mantegna and others. By then the artists were expanding their subject matter and making prints of lovers, of husbands and wives, of the sagas of knights and kings, and of the details of fetes and victories. There was a new liveliness of line, a pagan pleasure in drawing the nude body in repose or in action: battles of nude men, bacchanalian groups, sea gods at play.

In the centuries that followed, great artists like Brueghel, Rembrandt, Callot, Hogarth, Goya, Blake and Daumier were each to make some special artistic contribution to the excitement and skill of print making. In those times when few could read and news services did not exist, the print also served the purpose we now delegate to radio, television and motion pictures. From the time of Queen Anne on, popular broadsides and chapbooks of prints were hawked across the English countryside, and the demand was so great that today there are over eight thousand prints made from 1702 to 1800 in the British Museum's incomplete collection of the period.

By the middle of the nineteenth century, newspapers, the invention of photography, and more widespread education made prints less of a folk art, and the makers turned from the recording of current events to seeing the print as a work of art. Daumier still continued in the popular manner, fathering modern political caricature, but impressionists like Degas and Renoir, and other artists such as Toulouse-Lautrec and Gauguin, were involved in experimenting with the actual process of printing and with new styles. The beauty of line and the reproduction of fully finished drawings gave way to the dots, swirls and flakes of impressionism and the exploiting of the process of color lithography to the limit.

With the twentieth century and the artist's turning for inspiration to primitive forms, print making showed the influence of totems and ritual carvings, of the exploration of distorted reality. Then came Kandinski, who did away with representation of recognizable objects, while Klee reduced the expressionist print to a kind of Freudian scrawl. We are a long way from the first print makers, who were duty bound to be historians of their society and were much in love with the human body and its various postures and fashions. We are still too close to the abstractionists' work to make final judgments about it.

This book covers the ground as fully as one volume can, trying to show as many examples as possible of the various faces (or lack of

faces) the great prints have had. The selection, while personal to the author, is fairly well balanced between the old and the new. The twenty-three artists whose works are shown were in the main the true giants; other artists who also did beautiful and exciting prints have been crowded out. These are not, of course, *the* two hundred and thirty-two greatest prints in the world; to claim that they are would be foolish. But this collection does aim to give more than just a taste of the great print makers and their work.

HOW IT WAS DONE

THERE is no great mystery about print making. It takes some skill and technical ability to get the best prints from the plates or stones, but the best prints were often done with the simplest means and in the easiest manner.

In *etching,* the print is made from a copper plate which is either smoked or covered with hard varnish or wax; the artist can cut directly into the copper itself, or he can scratch through only the varnish with his etching tools. If he does the latter, acid is poured over the plate, and it bites through the exposed copper, eating out the lines not protected by the varnish. The artist can control the depth of the acid bite by the length of time he lets the chemical stay on the plate. By brushing part of the cleaned plate with acid he can get solid gray areas on the finished print. To print, the plate is cleaned and ink is spread on it and then wiped off except where it has filled in the sunken lines etched into the plate. A special damp paper is put over the plate and the two are run through a press, resulting in the image on the plate's being transferred onto the paper.

In making an *engraving* the engraver cuts his picture directly into a metal plate with special tools. The *woodcut*—a form of engraving— was the first popular type of print. The blocks of wood had an image cut into the surface with special knives; ink was rubbed on the surface and paper pressed against the damp surface. Fantastic skill was often shown by the woodcutters, who in most cases were not the artists of the design, but men who only cut other people's work. The prints of Dürer are magnificent examples of woodcutting, as are many of the Japanese prints.

Lithography is the newest print-making process, invented about 1796. It became popular in the early part of the nineteenth century as a cheap way of reproducing music scores which avoided going through the long, expensive process of engraving them on metal. Artists were quick to see its merits; Gillray and Goya both experimented with lithograph prints. Daumier created almost his entire life's work of prints, nearly four thousand of them, on the lithographer's stone. The process is based on the simple scientific discovery that oil and water do not mix. The artist makes his picture on a slightly grained white or gray stone, using a crayon made from grease and soot to draw his design. The stone is wet with water, and then over it is rolled a greasy ink which sticks only to the grease drawing. An impression can then be pulled on paper. Scores of impressions can be taken off a stone in this manner, for the process reproduces perfectly every small detail and variation of the original lithograph drawing. A well-pulled lithograph print with its solid blacks and light grays is an amazingly accurate reproduction of the artist's original. Woodcuts and lithographs are often made with extra color plates printed under the black key plate.

Collectors of prints are slightly mad on the subject of early states and condition. But to a lover of drawing and beauty, just a good, well-printed example is a delight. In time, plates wear down and the picture becomes shaggy and dark and thin in spots. The best bad examples are the once great plates of Goya that are still used in Spain, the results being almost worthless. On the other hand, any good shop selling old prints should be able to offer you, for a few dollars, a very good original lithograph by Daumier printed from his original stones—he did so many, and copies of the newspapers they appeared in are available. Original woodcuts after Winslow Homer can still be had in old copies of *Harper's Weekly.*

The other side of the shield is the fanatical collector in La Bruyère's *Caractères*, who laments, "I have no luck, and it's driving me to give up collecting for the rest of my life. I have everything Callot ever engraved but for one print. It's not even a good one; as a matter of fact, it's one of his worst things. But it would have completed my Callot collection. I've been slaving for twenty years to get that one print, but now I know I'm never going to find it. Of all the rotten luck!"

Stephen Longstreet

Elm Drive
California

The Prints and Their Makers

22

IN THE FIFTEENTH CENTURY, German graphic artists were producing mainly *Andachtsbilder*—holy images and religious woodcarvings and engravings—when there appeared Albrecht Dürer, whom the Germans have claimed as a great German artist ever since. A great artist, but not really a German; his father was a Magyar, who came from Hungary to set himself up as a goldsmith in Nuremberg and sired eighteen children in twenty-four years. The only one of them to become famous was born in 1471. Dürer spent his formative years as his father's apprentice, using graver and burin on prelates' spoons and landgraves' plates.

It was a northern land that he lived in, a land of solid, heavy men red-faced with wine and meat and preoccupied with the sensual love of the *teuflische Venus*. The rise of the Fuggers of Augsburg to a kind of Du Pont empire of trade and money and banking led to the collecting of art as a sign of prosperity. A good time for a young artist who slept badly and dreamed of the roster of trolls, gnomes, satyrs and kobolds that he was soon to engrave on copper; a sensitive, slender, delicate-looking boy—as his early self-portraits show—who studied the *Landsknechte* carousing in ale halls and the prelates selling the indulgences which were to be the immediate cause of Martin Luther's Reformation. It was the eve of a time of violent events—peasant uprisings, an increasing series of wars, the sacking of Rome. Dürer never fully shook off the cruelty of his time, but he was also drawn to the beauty of landscapes, budding plants, the hairy green grandeur of leafing trees, the rush and drip of mountain streams— even the fuzzy fur of a rabbit and the arch of senile hands held together in prayer.

In 1486 he had had enough of goldsmith work and was apprenticed to the painter and woodcarving-designer Michael Wolgemut, with whom he remained for three years, improving his use of pen, brush, gouache and water color and learning the secrets of oil painting and woodcutting. He admired the popular prints of Schongauer and the work of the Master of the Housebook. Soon he was off wander-

Dürer

GERMAN SCHOOL
1471-1528

2. DÜRER, The Adoration of the Magi

One of the few northern artists who could equal the work of the great Italian painters, Dürer was also the first great master of the woodcut. In this print he takes a popular medieval and Renaissance theme, places it in a setting free of the lushness of Rome, and creates a style of his own that points toward Rembrandt.

Woodcut, 11½" x 8⅝", courtesy of the Metropolitan Museum of Art, gift of Junius S. Morgan, 1919.

ing over Europe, the eternal German student, eying the habits and social graces of his neighbors. He saw the bestiality of the peasant and his great pride in his hogs. He enjoyed the beauty of the tapestried halls of archiepiscopal palaces.

In 1492 he was in Basel, a bookmaking center of Europe, where he practiced the illustrating of volumes set and printed on the bulky flatbeds of the period. Two years later he was back home in Nuremberg, where he seems to have been rushed into marriage by his family. There was a dowry of two hundred florins, but the marriage was not a success. Dürer's wife is supposed to have driven him to his death by overwork in the studio. For his part, he preferred the company of scholars and scientists—students of new discoveries—in the local *Stuben* to that of his wife. On journeys to great estates, she and her maid ate in the kitchen while Dürer, who could be elegantly epicurean, feasted with his host.

Dürer was drawn to the new humanism and to classical art. In the year of his dismal marriage he went to Italy alone. Bowing to the new cult of classical antiquity which was exciting all Italy, he studied the great artists' work and took what he needed from the ancients, then returned to Nuremberg and went to work. In a five-year period, from 1495 to 1500, he completed sixty engravings and woodcuts, complex and detailed, and much oil painting and many drawings. For sheer skill—and Dürer was a master engraver and a great draftsman—the technical perfection of these plates has never been equaled by another engraver. Their subject matter was mostly pious, but he also engraved peasants dancing, heads of emperors and princes, strange animals and freaks. In 1505 he was back in Italy, driven out of Nuremberg, it is claimed, by both a raging plague and his scolding wife.

He was a prodigious worker, like many other lonely, unhappy men, a scientist with a new version of perspective, a curious, probing artist aware that a new world was emerging from the ruins of religious wars and rebellions—perhaps not a better world, but at least a more exciting one. Dürer died in his fifties in 1528 as the result of overwork and, most likely, the malaria he caught on a trip to the Netherlands when he went into a mosquito-infested swamp to see the body of a whale that had reportedly been washed ashore. He left behind over a hundred famous engravings, two hundred and fifty superb woodcuts and over a thousand drawings. His grave is in the Johanneskirche cemetery in Nuremberg, under a simple marker:

DÜRER

3. DÜRER, Erasmus of Rotterdam

A balancing of detail with the art of portraiture. Erasmus comes through to us with all his
irony, but the eye is just as interested in the vase of flowers, the folds in the robe, the
details of the books. The parts are *the whole.*

Etching, 9²⁵⁄₃₅″ x 7½″, courtesy of the Metropolitan Museum of Art, Fletcher Fund, 1919.

QUIDQUID ALBERTI DURERI MORTALE FUIT
SUB HOC CONDITUR TUMULO

(Whatever was mortal of Albrecht Dürer is covered here)

DÜRER

He was a fine artist and the supreme engraving technician of his time. A complex, sensitive man, given to nightmares and visions, his was a Faustian nature, sold to a desire for perfection never attained. He studied the pre-Columbian arts of the Indians of the newly discovered Americas; he wrote treatises on perspective and human proportion. His great prints, "Melancholia I," the phantasmagorias of his illustrations for the Book of Revelations, the heavy German nudes he enjoyed etching (dumplings fertile as mink), show he was more than an artist interested in the surface of things. His cult of *Kunst* (knowledge) and *Brauch* (practice) was not the full secret of his genius. In his great print of Erasmus we see the two natures of the man of the Renaissance—the new humanism as opposed to the old faith. His print "The Knight, Death and the Devil" is one of his trembling dreams made real. The bloated physiognomies of his lords and bishops show more of a sense of humor than he is given credit for. It is in his most deep-felt moments that we see him at his best. *The Large Passion of Christ*, a series of prints amazing in their use of writhing, tormented line and his conceptions of anatomy, stars and landscape bring together the man and his time, the Age of Faith looking toward the Age of Reason.

Dürer drew from the world as he saw it and from Biblical texts that were as real to his time as newsreels are to ours. In this he was like Leonardo da Vinci, who wrote:

Seeing that I cannot choose any subject of great utility or pleasure because my predecessors have already taken as their own all useful and necessary themes, I will do like one who, because of his poverty, is the last to arrive at the fair and, not being able to do otherwise to provide himself, chooses all the things as being of little value. With these despised and rejected wares—the leavings of many buyers—I will load my modest pack, and therewith take my course, distributing, not amid the great cities, but among the mean hamlets, and taking such reward as befits the things I offer.

4.   DÜRER, The Knight, Death and the Devil

*The Devil and early death haunted Europe for centuries; only courage was the answer.
Using the symbols of his time, Dürer has depicted here the enigma of life and death as a
strange journey.*

Engraving, 9⅜" x 7⅜", courtesy of the Metropolitan Museum of Art, Dick Fund, 1934.

5. DÜRER, Adam and Eve

For Dürer, the human body was something to be studied with love, to be contemplated with neither shame nor a smirk. To the begetters of us all he gave his best shapes, and if the lady has slimmed down since, it is a change in fashion, not art, that has created the altered outline.

Engraving, 9⅞″ x 7⅝″, courtesy of the Metropolitan Museum of Art, Fletcher Fund, 1919.

6.   DÜRER, Melancholia I

Dürer had certain personal symbols which stood for those sad and heavy moments of life when no answer will do. We do not fully understand his symbols of melancholia, but the mood is clearly transmitted.

Engraving, 9½″ x 7⁵⁄₁₆″, courtesy of the Metropolitan Museum of Art, Dick Fund, 1943.

7. DÜRER, The Great Horse

This is not the beautiful horse the Greeks carved in marble or the horse the T'ang artists shaped in glazed clay. It is a very personal vision, one that could have been produced only by Dürer's needle.

Engraving, 6½″ x 4⅝″, courtesy of the Metropolitan Museum of Art, Fletcher Fund, 1919.

8. DÜRER, The Apocalypse: Saint Michael and His Angels

In a series of great woodcut prints for the Book of the Apocalypse, Dürer summed up the strife and emotional turmoil of his time, keying it to the texts of the Bible.

Woodcut, 15⅛″ x 10¹⁵⁄₁₆″, courtesy of the Metropolitan Museum of Art, gift of Junius S. Morgan, 1919.

9. DÜRER, The Riders on the Four Horses

This has been called the greatest print Dürer ever made. Certainly he made real to Europe how war, disease and greed could destroy mankind. His treatment vividly suggests Picasso's image of war's horrors, "Guernica."

Woodcut, 15¼" x 11", courtesy of the Metropolitan Museum of Art, gift of Junius S. Morgan, 1919.

10. DÜRER, Rhinoceros

Dürer never saw a rhinoceros, living or dead. From travelers' reports and early prints he made a true image, yet one that is all fantasy in its details.

Woodcut, 8⅜″ x 11⅝″, courtesy of the Metropolitan Museum of Art, gift of Junius S. Morgan, 1919.

11. DÜRER, The Cannon

With a more earthy realism, the artist shows one of the tools of war close up. The skill of Dürer as an etcher is fully exposed here. He mingles landscape, detail and people, handling the different textures with complete confidence.

Etching on iron, 8¹⁷⁄₃₂″ x 12¹⁹⁄₃₂″, courtesy of the Metropolitan Museum of Art, Fletcher Fund, 1919.

HE WAS KNOWN, we are told, as Peasant Brueghel, although no
proof has come down to us that Pieter Brueghel was of peasant
stock. He had two sons, also artists. They were known as Velvet
Brueghel (he painted soft and pleasant objects and scenes) and Hell
Brueghel (he pictured the hot red domains of the Devil). Brueghel
the Elder was a many-sided, overwhelming genius, painting heaven,
hell, religious scenes, proverbs, children's games, all kinds of genre
pictures of peasant life, landscapes, the four seasons, mythology,
allegory and animals.

The known facts about him are so meager that the nature of the
man must come to us from his prints and paintings. He was born,
according to the best guesswork, around 1525, and most likely in the
village of Brueghel, near Bree in the Limburg Campine, in what is now
the border area of Holland and Belgium. It was from that village that
the famous Flemish-Dutch artist took his name. In the nearby town
of 's Hertogenbosch the churches were still showing fearful masterpieces painted by Hieronymus Bosch, whose screaming demons, monsters and deformed souls influenced Brueghel's own early paintings.
Around 1545 Brueghel went to Antwerp and was apprenticed to Pieter
Coecke van Aelst, court painter to the Holy Roman Emperor Charles v.
The teacher had a beautiful baby daughter, and the young apprentice
carried her around the studio in his arms; he was later to marry her.

There is no information on his formative years. In 1551, it is recorded, Brueghel was admitted to the painters' guild of Antwerp. We
know that he left soon afterward for a journey to France and Italy, as
drawings of this trip have survived: Lyons, Vienna, Rome, then Naples
and Sicily, and back by the St. Gotthard Pass and the Martinswand,
near Innsbruck. He may have been sent on this journey by Hieronymus
Cock, who, under the sign "To the Four Winds," was the best-known
publisher of prints in the Netherlands. Certainly Brueghel began to
prepare drawings for Cock's engravers, and all his life the artist's
prints were issued with Cock's imprint. Brueghel, no trained engraver,
etched one landscape himself; the rest of his long series of magnificent

Brueghel

FLEMISH
1525(?)-69

Iulius, Auguſtus, nec non et Iunius Aeſtas ·   AESTAS Adoles tentię imago   Frugiferas aruis fert Aeſtas torrida meßeis ·

Not June, but July and August make the Summer
SUMMER, THE IMAGE OF YOUTH
In the heat of the Summer, the ploughed fields yield rich harvests.

12.   BRUEGHEL, Summer

Man lives in nature; in this magnificent drawing he is what he eats and drinks. Here Brueghel depicts a scene packed with Flemish vitality. Every line links the foreground figures with the wheat, the harvesters and the landscape, under a life-giving sun.

Engraving, 8¹⁵⁄₁₆″ x 11⁵⁄₁₆″, courtesy of the Metropolitan Museum of Art, Dick Fund, 1926.

prints were cut by the professional engraver at the Four Winds.

The remainder of Brueghel's life must have been the hard-working studio existence of an artist who was to die young and leave behind him many prints and drawings and over a dozen great paintings. We know that in 1563, in Brussels, he married his teacher's daughter, and that they had two sons. The next date we are sure of is 1569, when the artist died and was buried in Notre-Dame-de-la-Chapelle. There is a tradition that he was a calm man given to playing practical jokes on all around him. The engraving of him done by Aegidius Sadeler shows a substantial-looking longheaded gentleman with a magnificent, well-groomed beard and the sad, melancholy features of a philosopher much occupied with thoughts of life and death.

Brueghel's prints show us the inner world of his time—the phantoms, spooks and sins of man—as well as the landscapes and pleasures, the dances, the wedding feasts, the games of the country-side. His two best series of prints are *The Seven Vices* and *The Seven Virtues*. He was a Rabelaisian picturemaker crossed with a religious believer in the Devil and hell. He made of the beauty and the follies of this world both a personal image of nature and a map of the inner consciousness. The result was always a coherent picture of mankind divided between flesh and the spirit, between pride and the fall.

He worked in genre and allegory, enjoyed peasant life and the thinker's knowledge of the past; he mixed his stout profane earthy figures, guzzling, lusting, dancing, harvesting, with elegantly graceful Biblical characters that stand, sacred and alone, a little forward and away from what is happening in the rest of the picture. Brueghel loved crowds and he reveled in sketching them at a carnival, in battle, watching someone being crucified; people playing at games, rushing to a feast or lying on the ground after an orgy of eating and drinking. He took over the local saying, "All things become topsy-turvy in a topsy-turvy world" and showed how human nature in one period of history is in many ways like that in any other, including our own.

His overfed sensualists prone on the ground in his print "The Land of Cockaygne" are the same strong figures who work the fertile heated land in his "Harvesters." He was always sketching, hunting the basic core of human behavior, and he humbly signed his drawings *"Nart het leven"*—made from life.

Brueghel turned mysticism into intuition; he widened our experience to a rapt ecstasy in harmony with what was then known of the universe. Much more has been brought to our attention since, but some think it has only made our lives more shadowy, insubstantial and flavorless. Brueghel, on the other hand, made his world of gut and piety solid. His people are fully alive during their short existence in a time of plagues and wars. They dance quicker, they relish more the passing scene. The artist has them hunt that absolute which will contain all pain and all pleasure, all change and all time. Brueghel also hints at the infinite incomprehensibility that makes a mystery of things. He is one of the few artists whose works of art seem to contain audible voices of living people as well as forms and patterns.

BRUEGHEL

For that same sweet sin of lechery, I would say
    as the Friar said:
A young man and a young woman in a green arbor
    in a May morning—
If God do not forgive it, I would. . . .

SIR JOHN HARINGTON

MAGDALENA POENITENS·

ARTI ET INGENIO STAT SINE MORTE DECVS.

Pulcher Atlantiades Psychen ad Sydera tollens,
Ingenio scandi Sydera posse docet.

Ingenio liquidum possum conscendere Cælum,
Si mundi curas fata leuare velint.

Petrus Breugel fec: Romæ A: 1553.
Excud: Hous: cum præ Cæs:

THE GLORY OF ARTS AND GENIUS KNOWS NO DEATH

By carrying Psyche to the stars
Mercury, the Handsome, teaches that Genius may ascend to the stars

Were Fate to soothe the cares of the world,
I could equate Genius with the clear sky.

14. BRUEGHEL, Psyche with Mercury

His own land was flat and dull, but Brueghel's work is dominated by mountains and cliffs.
This was the result of a trip to Italy, which filled his mind with new images. In the fore-
ground, two artists are bent on recording a landscape while the messenger of the gods
flies by, bearing the Soul.

Engraving, 10⅝″ x 13⅜″, courtesy of the Metropolitan Museum of Art, Dick Fund, 1926.

13. BRUEGHEL, Penitent Magdalen

This artist was the first of the masters to make landscape an art in itself, not a mere back-
drop to people or events. Here he has gone so far in minimizing human activity that one
must search for the subject, which occupies only one small corner of the whole vital
composition.

Engraving, 12¾″ x 16¹³⁄₁₆″, courtesy of the Metropolitan Museum of Art, Dick Fund, 1926.

No one proud loves those above, nor is he loved by them.

Pride is hated by God above, and at the same time God is rejected by Pride.

15. BRUEGHEL, Seven Deadly Sins: Pride

The artist existed in two worlds: the medieval one of demons and sprites, and the earthy one of meat, drink and physical love. Here he gives us a welter of personal images, keeping order among his demons by a style that is clear and crisp.

Engraving, 8²⁷⁄₃₂″ x 11⅝″, courtesy of the Metropolitan Museum of Art, Dick Fund, 1926.

VIDENDVM, VT NEC VOLVPTATI DEDITI PRODIGI ET LVXVRIOSI
APPAREAMVS, NEC AVARA TENACITATI SORDIDI AVT OBSCVRI EXISTAMVS

It is up to us not to appear prodigal and dissolute in our dedication to pleasures, nor to live
sordidly or obscurely in our tenacious avarice.

16. BRUEGHEL, Seven Virtues: Temperance

*Each figure stands out clearly, and all who pass can read. Brueghel's world is far away
from ours, but we are closer to his models than we think.*

Engraving, 8¹³⁄₁₆″ x 11⁹⁄₁₆″, courtesy of the Metropolitan Museum of Art, Dick Fund, 1926.

FIDES MAXIMÈ À NOBIS CONSERVANDA EST PRAECIPVE IN RELIGIONEM, QVIA DEVS PRIOR ET POTENTIOR EST QVAM HOMO.

We must place the utmost faith in religion, since God is superior. . . .

17. BRUEGHEL, Seven Virtues: Faith

Brueghel did not engrave his own work. The artist was fortunate in having the printmaker Cock, whose skill helped to hold Brueghel's crowded pictures together without losing the force of the original drawings.

Engraving, 8⅞″ x 11⅝″, courtesy of the Metropolitan Museum of Art, Dick Fund, 1928.

INVIDIA HORRENDVM MONSTRVM, SÆVISSIMA PESTIS.
Een onsterffelijcke doot es nijt / en wreede peste Een beeft die haer feluen eet / met valfchen molefte

Envy is a horrible monster, an unbridled pestilence.

Envy is an unending death, an evil pestilence, a beast which wickedly feeds on itself.

18. BRUEGHEL, Seven Deadly Sins: Envy

Even if we accept these prints as surrealism, as pictures of a dream world that are never fully explained, they can be enjoyed as works of art, detailed and skillfully rendered.
Engraving, 8⅞″ x 11¹⁷⁄₃₂″, courtesy of the Metropolitan Museum of Art, Dick Fund, 1926.

SEGNITIES ROBVR FRANGIT, LONGA OCIA NERVOS.

Traechheyt maeckt machteloos / en verdrooght Die senuwen dat de mensch niewers toe en dooght

Sloth saps the strength, sooner or later undermines the sinews.
Sloth makes powerless and dries out the nerves so that Man is good for nothing.

19. BRUEGHEL, Seven Deadly Sins: Sloth

In many of these prints the artist escapes the clutches of the moralist, and we sense an instinctive use of space according to what the artist felt would make a good composition.
Engraving, 8 15/16″ x 11 19/32″, courtesy of the Metropolitan Museum of Art, Dick Fund, 1926.

H. cock excu.   PRVDENTIA   Brueg̈el   Inuentor

ŠI   PRVDENS   ESSE   CVPIS,   IN   FVTVRVM   PROSPECTVM   OSTENDE,   ET
QVAE   POSSVNT   CONTINGERE,   ANIMO   TVO   CVNCTA   PROPONE

If you wish to be prudent, display your outlook for the future and put in plain view all those
things that concern your soul.

20.   BRUEGHEL, Seven Virtues: Prudence

*Modern critics who have a fear of objective content can enjoy this plate for the grace of
its figures and the handling of its patterns. Notice how the bundles of faggots and the
flayed ox have become pure forms, free of realism.*

Engraving, 8⅞″ x 11⅝″, courtesy of the Metropolitan Museum of Art, Dick Fund, 1928.

SCOPVS LEGIS EST, AVT VT EV̄ QVĒ PVNIT EMENDET, AVT POENA
EIVS CAETEROS MELIORES REDDET AVT SVBLATIS MALIS CAETERI SECVRIŌRES VIVAT̄.

It is the purpose of the law either to correct the one it punishes or to make others better through
his punishment, or to make life more secure for others by eliminating the evil.

21. BRUEGHEL, Seven Virtues: Justice

*Brueghel probably had his misgivings about the cruel forms that "justice" took in his day,
but formal respect is still shown here for judges, lawyers and jailers. Years later, Daumier
and Rouault would tear off the masks and show what lay beneath.*
Engraving, 8⅞" x 11⅝", courtesy of the Metropolitan Museum of Art, Dick Fund, 1928.

46

LVXVRIA ENERVAT VIRES, EFFOEMINAT ARTVS.

Luxurÿe stinckt / sÿ is vol onsuuerheden Sÿ breeckt die Crachten / en sÿ swackt die leden

Lechery stinks, it is full of uncleanness, it breaks the powers and weakens the limbs.
Lust undermines strength, weakens the limbs.

22.   BRUEGHEL, Seven Deadly Sins: Lust

Moral values were not sugar-coated and graphic art did not hide behind style in Brueghel's art. The artist here retains the purity of a historian recording a secret side of society's behavior.

Engraving, $8\frac{31}{32}''$ x $11\frac{21}{32}''$, courtesy of the Metropolitan Museum of Art, Dick Fund, 1928.

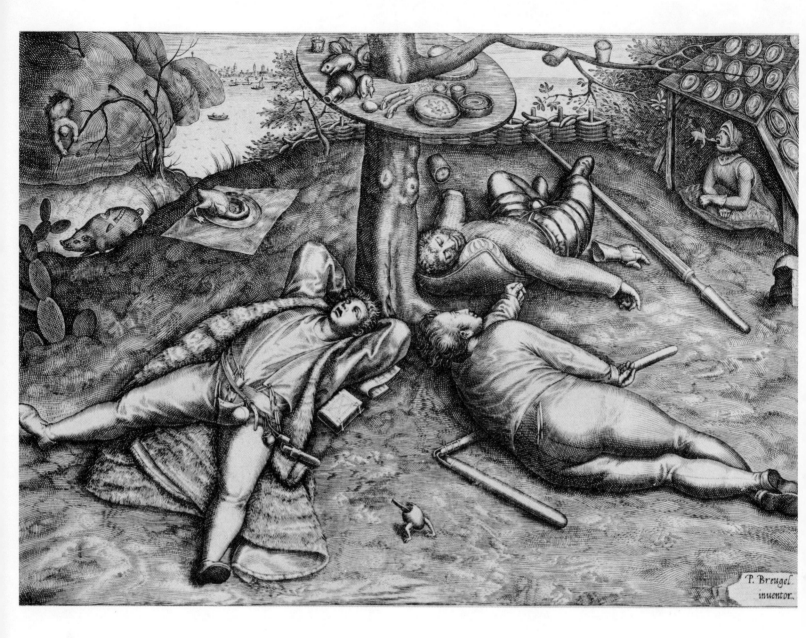

23.   BRUEGHEL, Luilekkerland, or The Land of Cockayne

Luilekkerland was for the people of Brueghel's time, and even for Dutch children today, an imaginary country where the rivers run orangeade, sausages grow in the garden and roofs are tiled with pies. As the caption says, everything is deliciously edible and no one has to lift a finger. You can get there only by eating your way through a mountain of rice pudding (note figure on left). In this print, Brueghel has left behind his dream world of demons for one of inexhaustible goodies; both are frightening in their different ways, for in a land where larks fly roasted into the mouth, what will men become?

Engraving, 9³⁄₃₂″ x 11²⁹⁄₃₂″, courtesy of the Metropolitan Museum of Art, Dick Fund, 1926.

THE FIRST MODERN ETCHER of genius, Jacques Callot, was born at Nancy, in the independent duchy of Lorraine, in the last decade of the sixteenth century–the generally accepted year is 1592.

The age he lived in was a time of transition, the Counter-Reformation era, marked by devastating wars in which two Christian parties fought each other, burned, pillaged and slaughtered–each in the name of the one true God. There were the Wars of Religion in neighboring France in the day of Henry IV, and the Thirty Years' War in Germany in the day of Richelieu and Gustavus Adolphus, Wallenstein and Tilly. It was also the age of baroque art–Rubens and Velázquez; of the flowering of the drama–Shakespeare, Ben Jonson, Corneille; of the dawn of science and reason–Galileo and Descartes.

Callot caught it all: the miseries of war, the pomp and the splendor, the streets and the fairs, beggars and gypsies, cavaliers, acrobats, dwarfs. He studied mathematics with Galileo and even essayed trigonometry. He saw the world as a theater and pictured the *comédie humaine* with both integrity and style. In a short life of forty-two years he did more than 1,500 prints with a grace and an elegance that make tormented men seem to be part of a ballet, make the hangman himself seem to move as gracefully as a Nijinsky.

Callot's father was a minor official in the court of the Duke of Lorraine. His four brothers were all monks, his sister was a nun; he, the unruly son, was apprenticed in the glass-painting studio of the Henriot family. When a friend wrote from Italy of the wonders to be found in the studios there, Callot decided to follow him.

Most art historians accept the story that when he was twelve or thirteen he ran away from home and joined a band of gypsies going south. He lived with them for several months, and his memories of their lean, smoky outdoor life are recorded in his four famous prints *Les Bohémiens*. Arriving at length in Florence, he became an apprentice at the studio of Cantagallina, fireworks engineer and painter to the Medici, but later, in Rome, he was picked up by friends from home and shipped back to his family. A year or so after returning he again

24.   CALLOT, Pantaloon

One of the most remarkable of Callot's great prints. He has captured the strut and pose of the actor-clown, all the phony grandeur and deliberate illusion of the theater. It is an oblique communion across the footlights, but it gives us the feeling that we know this man and his world fully.

Engraving, 9½″ x 6″, courtesy of the Metropolitan Museum of Art, bequest of Edwin de T. Bechtel, 1957.

ran away to Italy, and now a monkish brother had him sent home. Two years later, this time with his family's blessing, he was officially in Rome, working in the studio of Philippe Thomassin, drawing, engraving and etching like a young master, influenced by the prints of Bosch, Brueghel and Lucas van Leyden and by Leonardo da Vinci's caricatures.

In 1611 Callot moved to Florence, where he spent a wonderful ten years, first with the Medici as patrons; they gave him room and board and studio space and listed him as "Jacques Castor de Lorraine, *graveur au burin*." During this period he produced some of his greatest plates. He created a drama in print form, his first version of "The Temptation of Saint Anthony"; also the print "The Great Fair at Impruneta," and the clowns and mountebanks of the Commedia dell' Arte, the Italian folk theater. In 1621 he was back at the Lorraine court, where he married the daughter of a nobleman; a writer called her "acquisitive and prudent."

It was often a remarkably gay and active Europe that Callot knew, with its crowded harbors and market places, its fairs and parades. It was also a mosaic of states attacked and defended by hard, hired faces under steel casques, marching Swiss pikemen, German lansquenets casually firing their muskets with the new flintlocks. It was a world where the discipline and renunciation of monastic life contrasted sharply with the appetites of princes magnificently endowed with the rewards of the world, each claiming to be the *Fidei Defensor*, Defender of the Faith.

Callot went down to the market and the fair, stood in palaces at fetes and put it all down in his perfect little plates. His men in plumed hats and his women in their trailing silk are real, and they could really react to life

> *. . . as when a grace*
> *Sprinkles another laughing face*
> *With nectar and runs on.*

If he also drew grotesque dwarfs and scenes of torture, it was because he saw his world at all levels. The freshness of his style, the charm of his drawings, the pure line of detail made him a kind of historical novelist of the seventeenth century. The artist was still permitted then to reflect the passing scene, report the events and the pageants that made up his world. Today a different fashion dictates to our artists, yet the work of Callot influenced the world of picturemaking for several centuries.

In 1625 Callot went to the Low Countries, where he did a series of huge plates of the siege of Breda, a kind of motion picture of the men engaged, the broken landscape and the smoking battleground. Later he set down his version of the condition of man as an undomesticated animal in his *Miseries of War,* a set of etchings that were the first to depict historically the basic cruelty of man against man. The Thirty Years' War was only half over when he did them, but it is all here. There is no sterile aesthetics on the stage where these fearful dramas are played out. The artist's line is strong, direct; there is no smell of the Middle Ages; it is modern art.

CALLOT

We see Callot himself in Vorsterman's engraving of him, after a lost painting by Vandyck. It is a delicate, witty face, presenting to the world a calm exterior, a courtly manner, but showing signs of illness; he suffered much from the disease of modern big business, stomach ulcers, and tried to live in what a later writer was to call "grace under pressure." The artist went on working till the end, etching saints and beggars and town scenes—he did some of the earliest known views of the Paris streets. His line and style influenced Goya and Tiepelo, and his drawings of *gueux*—beggars—were the basis of Rembrandt's style when he began etching.

It was most likely a perforated ulcer that brought Callot to his deathbed in 1635. His monument in a local church was destroyed when a wall fell in, but hundreds of his actual copper plates still exist, and all his prints. The artist would have approved the words of an admirer of his work, Goethe, who said, "Whenever I have a sorrow I make a poem." Callot etched a plate: a dance of the hours, lovers, the Bacchic rout or courtly revels. One hears the cymbals and flutes in his work, catches glimpses of pagan antiquity re-dressed in modern garb; it is the best of the Renaissance passed on to the coming centuries.

25. CALLOT, Temptation of St. Anthony

If Callot's work points forward to Rembrandt, it also looks back to Brueghel. We might see this scene as a kind of macabre fantasy, a sort of Halloween vision, but in Callot's time most people were ready to believe that such creatures actually existed. As an engraving this is a masterwork; for our present taste it seems overcrowded.

Etching, 14 1/16″ x 18 1/8″, courtesy of the Metropolitan Museum of Art, gift of Henry Walters, 1917.

Israel excud. cum Priuil. Reg.

Ce n'est pas sans raison que les grands Cappitaines	Contre les faineants, et les Blasphemateurs	De qui les actions par le vice aueuglées
Comme bien aduisez, ont inuente ces peines	Traistres a leur deuoir, querelleux, et menteurs	Rendent celles d'autruy laches et desreglées. 10

It is not without reason that the great Captains	**Against the slothful, and the Blasphemers**	**Whose actions, by vice blinded,**
Well-advisedly invented these penalties	**Traitors to their duty, quarrelsome, and liars**	**Render those of others cowardly and disordered.**

26. CALLOT, Miseries of War

In depicting the horrors of war, Callot could not shed his stylishness and courtly elegance. The figures have grace, no matter how tormented, and the scene looks more like a moment in some tragic opera than grim reality. It would take Goya and Daumier to show that war must not be seen as a kind of grand game.

Engraving, 4¼″ x 8½″, courtesy of the Metropolitan Museum of Art, Rogers Fund, 1922.

Israel ex. Cum Priuil: Reg.

Ces ennemis du Ciel qui pechent mil fois	Font gloire mechamment de piller et d'abattre	Mais pour punition de les auoir brulez,
Contre les saincts Decrets et les diuines Loix	Les Temples du vray Dieu d'vne main idolatre;	Ils sont eux mesmes enfin aux flammes immolez. 13

These enemies of Heaven who sin a thousand times
Against the holy Decrees and the divine Laws

Wickedly boast of pillaging and casting down
The Temples of the true God with an idolatrous hand;

But as punishment for having burned them down,
They themselves are finally immolated in the flames.

27. CALLOT, Miseries of War

Brutality in the artist's time was cloaked in ceremony which concealed the true madness of war. Yet this callous posing does not reflect Callot's personal view; the period as a whole was indifferent to human suffering in a way unmatched until the years of the German concentration camps.

Engraving, 4³⁄₁₆″ x 8⁵⁄₁₆″, courtesy of the Metropolitan Museum of Art, Rogers Fund, 1922.

L'œil touſiours ſurueillant de la diuine Aſtrée
Bannit entierement le dueil d'vne contrée.

Lors que tenant l'eſpeé, et la Balance en main
Elle iuge et punit le voleur inhumain,

Qui guette les paſſans, les meurtrit, et ſen ioüe,
Puis luy meſme deuient le ioüet d'vne roüe. 14

The ever-watchful eye of the divine Astraea
Entirely banishes mourning from a country,

Who lurks in wait for passers-by, murders them and mocks them,
Then himself becomes the plaything of a wheel.

When holding the Sword and the Scales in her hands
She judges and punishes the inhuman thief

28. CALLOT, Miseries of War

One is amazed at the small size of these prints, reproduced here in their original measurements. So much is included, yet there is no feeling of crowding. The artist stages his scene perfectly, with a foreground, middleground for the action, and background in the proper mood.

Engraving, 4¼″ x 8¼″, courtesy of the Metropolitan Museum of Art, Rogers Fund, 1922.

Voyla les beaux exploits de ces cœurs inhumains
Ils rauagent par tout rien ne chappe à leur mains

L'vn pour auoir de l'or, iauente des ſupplices,
L'autre à mil forfaicts anime ſes complices ;

Et tous d'vn meſme accord commettent mechamment
Le vol, le rapt, le meurtre, et le violement. 5

Behold the fine exploits of these inhuman hearts
They ravage everywhere, nothing escapes their hands

And all with one accord wickedly commit
Theft, abduction, murder and rapine.

One, to gain gold, invents tortures,
Another to a thousand misdeeds excites his accomplices;

29. CALLOT, Miseries of War

Here Callot almost frees himself from the attitudes and manners of his time and gives us a scene of unleashed horror. The soldiers commit rape, torture, murder, without benefit of pomp and circumstance.

Engraving, 4⅛″ x 8³⁄₁₆″, courtesy of the Metropolitan Museum of Art, Rogers Fund, 1922.

Israel ex. cum privil. Regis.

Voyez, que c'est du monde et combien de hazars
Persecutent sans fin les enfans du Dieu Mars

Les vns estropiez, se treinent sur la terre
Les autres plus heureux se sleuent a la guerre

Les vns sur vn gibet meurent d'vn coup fatal,
Et les autres s'en vont du Camp a L'Hospital. 15

See how it is with the world and how many hazards
Endlessly persecute the children of the God Mars

Some, crippled, drag themselves along the ground
Others more fortunate steal away at war

Some on a gibbet die of a fatal blow,
And others go from the Camp to the Disabled Soldiers' Home.

30. CALLOT, Miseries of War

People in Callot's day had the time in which to view slowly and relish elaborate settings. The print maker was expected to do more than re-create the mood of an event; he also had to show actual surroundings and fill his plate with much detail. The legless and armless cripples in this print evoke no horror—they are actors in a grand composition.

Engraving, 4³⁄₁₆″ x 8¼″, courtesy of the Metropolitan Museum of Art, Rogers Fund, 1922.

Israel ex. cum Privil. Reg.

Apres plusieurs degast par les soldats commis
A la fin les Paisans, qu'ils ont pour ennemis

Les guettent à l'escart et par vne surprise
Les ayant mis à mort les mettent en chemise,

Et se vengent ainsi contre ces Malheureux
Des pertes de leurs biens, qui ne viennent que d'eux 17

After havoc wrought several times by the soldiers
Finally the Peasants, whose enemies they are

Lay in wait for them out of the way, and by surprise
Having put them to death, strip off their clothing

And thus avenge themselves upon these Miserable Ones
For the loss of their goods, which comes only from them.

31. CALLOT, Miseries of War

It is fashionable to speak of modern artists having solved aesthetic problems that their predecessors did not even suspect existed. Yet the composition here, in which the artist has used the men's spears to form patterns of interlocking triangles, is very similar to Cézanne's handling of trees in his great paintings of the bathers. Today, this type of composition is common practice; in Callot's time, it was not.

Engraving, 4⅛″ x 8⁵⁄₁₆″, courtesy of the Metropolitan Museum of Art, Rogers Fund, 1922.

Vous qui prenez plaisir en leurs parolles,
Gardez uos blancs, uos testons, et pistolles.

You who take pleasure in their words,/Keep our pennies, dubloons and pistoles.

32.   CALLOT, The Bohemians

The skill of the engraving, the eloquent delicacy of line, show us the artist at his best. These gypsies have survived time and style; no part of the plate lacks its little drama.
Engraving, 6⅜″ x 10⅜″, courtesy of the Metropolitan Museum of Art, Rogers Fund, 1922.

Ne uoila pas de braues messagers
Qui uont errants par pays estrangers.

Are those not brave messengers/Who go wandering through foreign lands

33.   CALLOT, The Bohemians

A delightful print of gypsies on the march. Callot made finished drawings for many of his prints and never attempted to transpose his material directly onto the plate. He refined everything into style.
Engraving, 6⅜″ x 10⅞″, courtesy of the Metropolitan Museum of Art, Rogers Fund, 1922.

57

34.   CALLOT, View of Pont Neuf

Callot was among the first to do a landscape as a picture in its own right. The stiff, unreal scenery of early woodcuts is here replaced by vistas and façades rising in real air, smudged with smoke and worn by weather, animated by living men and animals.

Engraving, 6½″ x 13¼″, courtesy Metropolitan Museum of Art, gift of Theodore de Will, 1923.

TO THE MOST SERENE COSMO THE GREAT, RULER OF ETRURIA

A great many people attend the Impruneta Fair at the time of the Feast of St. Luke and much Merchandise is sold in front of the famous church built by the noble family of Bondelmonte. In the church there is an image of the Virgin Mother, painted by St. Luke.

THERE ARE HUNDREDS of good artists produced in every century, and talented ones in great herds. But the true creator, the original mover who cuts deeply into the river bed of art with a new channel, appears only a few times in any era. Such a man was born on a Dutch country lane beside the Oude Rijn River in 1606, a miller's son: Rembrandt Harmensz (or Harmenszoon) van Rijn. His father ground malt for beer; he had six dull brothers, a sad sister, and a simple Bible-reading mother. Why a genius should have sprung from such a placid setting is one of the mysteries of nature that have not yet been explained.

The boy early began to sketch the mill, the winding river, the flat green landscape that held back the cold North Sea. At fourteen he was a student at the University of Leyden, which he listlessly attended for a year and where he proved that he was no student of books. He was then apprenticed—a large, eager country bumpkin—to a bad painter named van Swanenburgh, and later to one called Lastman. Rembrandt was original; these men were not. But the tough, brusque young man learned his trade so well that by 1625 he was an independent master in Leyden, doing conventional overdressed portraits and the Bible subjects whose drama attracted him. He was living the life of a healthy young man on the town.

The Netherlands of Rembrandt's day was a market place of cheese and herring, lumber, good honest woolen cloth and gold coins changing hands. It was a time of prosperity in a country now virtually free from the horror of the Holy Office and from rule by a cruel Spanish king. The artists who could picture its fat women, rosy, well-stuffed children, *mijnheer* in his ruff and military uniform or guild honors, were the men to hire. The love of good dining led to a love of table-top paintings, of reproducing in detail fine wineglasses, sleek, dewy fruit, the glint of candlelight on ivory knife handles; a small world of digestion dominated by roasted game or glassy-eyed fish. Painters flourished, making little masterpieces from ample supplies of calories.

Rembrandt

DUTCH
1606-69

35. CALLOT, The Great Fair at Impruneta

Callot is the first of the modern etchers and engravers. He has turned from the contemporary obsession with the Church and royalty to the world around him. In this picture of the great fair, he leaves nothing out; yet his detail never bores us.

Engraving, 16 15/16" x 26¼", courtesy of the Metropolitan Museum of Art, Dick Fund, 1917.

REMBRANDT

Rembrandt, however, concentrated on Dutch faces and poses rather than native cheeses. An early work was the famous "Anatomy Lesson," in which a group of local surgeons watch the professor dissect the brachial tendons of a cadaver. This painting made the young artist famous enough to move him on to the big city of Amsterdam. He prospered there, for Rembrandt even in his early heavy style was the stuff of genius. His work showed a new kind of realism, not posed or stillborn but fully alive, as if a scene were glimpsed by accident through a door. The viewer of his work participated in the scene, came face to face in portraiture with the well-fed merchant stomachs and the proud mustaches. Basing his work on his many drawings, a calligraphic style of darting, lively lines, of changing rhythm, Rembrandt was no academic mannerist. Eager and earnest, by 1629 he was experimenting with new keys to art, moving out beyond the safe formulas of popular pictures to a chiaroscuro of his own.

Rembrandt began to make crude etchings on copper of himself, of his mother, of beggars. He began to work in Caravaggio's new realism, with faces carved boldly into light and shade, startling highlights contrasting features hidden in darkness. His prints also showed his new ideas in art—"The Beheading of John the Baptist," and several Christs. Never before had there been such vitality in prints, yet they were so native to the cold north. Some of his early plates look as if he drew with the blunt end of a nail directly through his stopping varnish.

Fascinated by etching, Rembrandt brought into his studio Joris van Vliet, a professional etcher, who worked on many of the large Rembrandt plates of the period. The tousled, unbuttoned artist did dozens of versions of his own shaggy head, of himself dressed up as a fine gentleman or with his artist's cap set on one side, of himself staring directly at his own image. He also did such things as the startling composition of "The Raising of Lazarus."

By 1632 Rembrandt was high in popular esteem, and two years later he married Saskia van Uylenburgh, of a substantial middle-class family superior to his own miller's background. She was a plump young woman and her appeal to Rembrandt is suggested by the honest nudes the artist etched, which seem lumpy to our own more sleek age. Inspired by her generous form, he made a print of a gloriously fat-ribbed Adam and Eve. There was in Rembrandt a kind of honest, sweating sensuality that one finds in the peasant orgies of Brueghel.

Saskia made him happy; he lived well in a large house, he collected

36. REMBRANDT, Rembrandt Leaning on a Stone Sill

Portrait of the artist as a young genius. The eyes are amused; the rest of the trappings—including the well-turned mustache and beard—are pure theater. This is a young man full of pride: Job before the boils.

Etching, 8⅛″ x 6⁷⁄₁₆″, courtesy of the National Gallery of Art, gift of R. Horace Gallatin.

37. REMBRANDT, Descent from the Cross by Torchlight

Rembrandt has been called the greatest of all etchers. Possessed of poetic instinct, he struck out boldly in new directions. In this tragic masterwork we see the profundity of his vision.

Etching, 8¼″ x 6⁷⁄₁₆″, courtesy of the Metropolitan Museum of Art, gift of Felix M. Warburg, 1917.

38. REMBRANDT, Christ with the Sick Around Him, Receiving Little Children
(The "Hundred Guilder" Print)

It is a comment on our way of life that the price of this print, when first pulled, has become its title to some. The print gains its profundity and significance from those dark featureless masses out of which the subject matter burns incandescently, like a vision.

Etching, 15½" x 11⅟₁₆", courtesy of the National Gallery of Art, Rosenwald Collection.

39. REMBRANDT, Woman Sitting Beside a Stove

The artist did not see woman in terms of classic beauty or perfect proportions. He could not make of the nude a specious, standardized product. Here he takes a Dutch housemaid, heavy, fertile and mortal, and gives her a solid grace worthy of a goddess.

Etching, 8⅞″ x 7⅜″, courtesy of the National Gallery of Art, Rosenwald Collection.

art. And art objects: armor, china, swords, costumes—he was the prey of dealers in this fancy trash. But his wife was not well. Illness was soon printed on her features, and he drew her sick in bed, staring ahead at eternity. In 1641 a son, Titus, was born to them. A few months later Saskia was dead, and her grieving husband was sketching in swift dry point a delicate dedicated plate, "The Death of the Virgin."

The best people no longer went to him for their portraits. Narrow-minded society found his life irregular. The fates and the furies had Rembrandt now, this materialist, the lover of fat living, of silk and velvets and jewels. His great "Night Watch" (really a day picture overvarnished, and now overcleaned) was rejected by the company of sporting townsmen who had ordered it. Rembrandt damned them and sank into quiet neglect as more and more turned against him. A woman servant sued him for intimate reasons, and a new maid appeared. Hendrickje Stoffels was young, ardent and unable to read or write. In her Rembrandt found someone to love, but this did not keep him from going deeper into debt and closer to bankruptcy as creditors closed in.

Rembrandt was past the few attempts at coarse popularization he had tried in painting, which were mostly atelier work. He had done much good work in prints. The baroque "Descent from the Cross," the so-called Thirty-Guilder and Twenty-Guilder prints (because of the high prices they sold for) had been successful. Now neglected, he was cutting deeper into the copper his personal impressions and emotions. Perhaps it was this independent search that helped destroy him in the society that had once raised him up. It was a world impressed by commercial gain, pious on the surface, critical of manners and smug with pride. The burghers' taste was not Rembrandt's now; the Dutch resented the artist and then forgot him.

He went to nature for print material, without studio help (he now did his plates alone)—went to the landscape, the mills, the old trees, the hunter and his dogs. He captured the straw roofs of the peasant houses, the canals and the brooding sky and the flat, flat land. Rembrandt combined nature and imagination in powerful lion hunts. He made long, narrow prints, panoramic views of Dutch cities sunk in the tidal muds. He etched "Christ Healing the Sick" and "Ecce Homo." He cut into his prints the humble splendor, the dazzling light of Him who had not failed the artist. Alone, Rembrandt put nuances of atmosphere into his prints, as no one had before. His landscapes were cut with a

REMBRANDT

40. REMBRANDT, The Goldweigher's Field

Any print is basically an interplay of lines. Here, Rembrandt has added just enough to indicate a field and houses on a wet horizon, trees following a canal. But he was fully aware of when to stop; we see then that he has made over nature in a new way.
Etching, 4¾″ x 12¹¹⁄₁₆″, courtesy of the National Gallery of Art, Rosenwald Collection.

broad, irregular burr and were almost impressionistic; the sweeping contours of his lines showed he was beyond the art of his time. Of pastoral nature he made lyric poems, works mature, serene. And from his mother's Bible he made biting, tearing dramas that were closer to the truth than the fancy church art.

In 1653 Rembrandt was hopelessly in debt, and ruin was close. Four years later he was bankrupt; everything went—his property, his pictures, his art collections. All he was permitted to keep were some of his etching plates. His debtors hounded him so that he signed a contract with Hendrickje and his son Titus to work for them as their employee.

He was old now, and the faces he etched and painted of himself were wilder, the eyes deep in wrinkled flesh filled with sadness; both youth and middle age were gone. So was the coarse imitation of a cavalier with the potato nose of a healthy peasant. The swollen, creased and raddled flesh of age took its place. Gone was the jolly animalism. Con-

sciousness, a deep awareness of tragedy, now looked out from the puffy eyes. Disconsolate and in neglect, he worked on. Habit makes life tolerable.

Time, contemplation and genius met and merged in the artist. His prints speak of the compulsion he had to record every change in his features as wisdom and understanding came to him. Rembrandt drew personal evanescent images, the unique, unself-conscious emotions. Now he did other nudes—not the smoky flesh of his youth, but classical forms, calm, unsensual. The etchings he made were tragically magnificent, and his last masterpieces were direct, honest battles of light and dark, of mind and matter. The Christs, the milling crowds, the forms of nature were now unique, universal, beyond his time. They also rank him with the peers of line of his day: Rubens, Callot. Rembrandt too was of the great draftsmen.

In a chaos that ended by bewitching his art, he lived on among the bearded Jewish patriarchs in their rags, on the fringe of the ghetto, working in his colored muds or on his etchings, trying again and again to capture the last majesty of flesh and ideas, a poet of Scriptural earnestness forgotten by the world of *staalmeesters.*

"What I want," he said, as he chewed on some salt herring and sipped his gin, "is not honors but freedom."

He had it, the freedom of neglect and indifference. Freedom to go on investing the pitiable and noble condition of man with spiritual light, and thereby produce some of the great prints of the world.

In 1665 Rembrandt did his last etchings. The final, peering portrait shows a decaying, bloated old man with red-rimmed eyes and a rum-blossom nose. His sight must have been failing; he scratched less on the etching copper, made the bite of the burr in looser and looser patterns that yet never faltered. Then he stopped etching. Hendrickje died, his son died.

It was all in the past now, the gay years of worldly success, the slovenly informality of a ménage isolated by Dutch disfavor. Soon he would be gone from the shared life of old-clothes merchants in their slum. Art had for Rembrandt a duty to present some clue to the hope of the universe, to the invisible world of ideas and things spiritual. Art, he now knew, was nature and man's ideas, seen through the distilling temperament of genius. One of the wise old Jews who still respected him had said to him something the Greeks once wrote: "To marvel is the beginning of knowledge. When we cease to marvel we cease to know."

Rembrandt died in 1669, dourly remembered by the art guilds and by a few mourning pupils, but in great public neglect. The businesslike ledger of the Westerkerk records his passing as ". . . bier with 17 bearers . . . fee, 20 guilders."

He had once said, "A picture is finished when the artist has fulfilled his purpose in undertaking to do it."

41.   REMBRANDT, Landscape with Hay Barn and Flock of Sheep

The old masters neglected landscape except as occasional background for their pictures. Rembrandt was one who made of trees and houses, fields and sky, a picture as telling as any nude, as majestic as any king.

Etching, 3⁹⁄₁₆″ x 7¼″, courtesy of the National Gallery of Art, Rosenwald Collection.

42.   REMBRANDT, View of Amsterdam

Whistler was to learn much from Rembrandt's landscapes. Atmospheric effects now seem easy; the formidable eye of the Dutch artist clarified for us the look of a city resting on a flat plain.

Etching, 4⁹⁄₁₆″ x 6⅛″, courtesy of the National Gallery of Art, Rosenwald Collection.

43.   REMBRANDT, Great Jewish Bride

This is the first state—a first impression from the plate while still in work—of one of Rembrandt's best prints. He has captured his subject, and she sits attenuated by an inexplicable grace. Now he will refine his picture and fill in its background and details.

Etching, 8¹¹⁄₁₆″ x 6⅝″, courtesy of the National Gallery of Art, Rosenwald Collection.

44. REMBRANDT, Great Jewish Bride

This is the fourth state of the same subject. The artist has added strong lines, he has drawn a body and hands. The background is firmer and richer. We have before us the tribal secret of survival: the bride and future mother.

Etching, 8½″ x 6½″, courtesy of the National Gallery of Art, Rosenwald Collection.

45.   REMBRANDT, The Large Lion Hunt

This print is not encumbered by banal details. Rembrandt has drawn directly on the plate.
But while everything looks accidental, notice how all the diagonals—spears and swords—
move down across the print and how the arrow in the dying beast stands out at a right
angle against them.

Etching, 8¾″ x 11¹³⁄₁₆″, courtesy of the National Gallery of Art, Rosenwald Collection.

46.   REMBRANDT, Faust in His Study Watching a Magic Disc

The artist had many functions, Rembrandt felt. One was to sever the nerve ends that connect us with reality. Here the subject jeopardizes ordinary sanity while invoking a higher sensibility. There are no demons, no underworld smoke, no sense of false theater. The artist, like Faust himself, remains calm.

Etching, 8¼″ x 6⁵⁄₁₆″, courtesy of the National Gallery of Art, Rosenwald Collection.

48. REMBRANDT, Landscape with Trees, Farm Buildings and a Tower

The artist's skill is deceptive. We are not aware of the plan at first, of how purposefully he has set the dark mass of trees against the lighter branches, the fully detailed roof against the other out-buildings. Long before the revelations of abstract art, Rembrandt knew what comprised the true bones of a composition.

Etching, 5⅝" x 13", courtesy of the National Gallery of Art, Rosenwald Collection.

47. REMBRANDT, Landscape with Cottage and a Large Tree

Rembrandt did not need battle scenes or high life for subject matter. He could make a vital and vivid picture from such humble elements as a muddy canal bank, a house crouched under an old tree, and the wide sweep of the horizon.

Etching, 5⅛″ x 13″, courtesy of the National Gallery of Art, Rosenwald Collection.

49.   REMBRANDT, Thomas J. Haaring ("The Young Haaring")

*No wonder Rembrandt lost his well-paying portrait business. Here, with
the Elizabethan poet, he sees "the skull beneath the skin." Overt melancholy is caught by a few scratched lines.*

Etching, 7¾″ x 6″, courtesy of the National Gallery of Art, Rosenwald Collection.

SOME ARTISTS struggle for many years to discover what their true world is, how they can best convey their impression of it when they have decided, and how to cast their vision of that world in a permanent art form. William Hogarth was spared this search, for he was born in the middle of his life's work and subject matter: in Bartholomew Close, London, in the year 1697, within view of Newgate Prison, of fairgrounds, markets and hospital, and just next door to Mr. Downinges the printer.

It was a bustling world turned away from Puritan repressions of pleasure to an outright expression of vitality and delight in living. The Lord Mayor imposed an ordinance for "the suppression of vicious practices . . . obscene, lascivious and scandalous plays and comedies" which was aimed at controlling activities in the town and particularly at the fair. But not too much attention was paid to ordinances.

Young Hogarth grew up to the sound of merry-andrews, to the ranting of tragedians on open-air platforms at Bartholomew Fair. The glitter of pewter mugs and gilded leather buskins, the flapping of banners, all gladdened his first impressions. The Guild of Merchant Taylors— in the days of male peacocks—strutted past his father's house; also the pickpockets, the vendors of roast pork and of small beers bittered with colocynth, the balladmongers peddling broadsides about the latest highwayman hanged out Tyburn way. Young William surely had a penny trumpet and most likely had a "Bartholomew baby" to play with; the word *doll* had not yet been applied to the toy.

The first objects of art he observed must have been the emblematic figures of Liberty, Security and Peace on one wall of Newgate Prison, Justice, Plenty and Fortitude on the other. The effluvium from this prison was famous, and the reeking felons, jailed for debt, small crimes (punished by hanging) and highway robbery, were exploited by their jailers. Yet they often became heroes as, on the road to the gallows, they sat upon coffins, swilling gin, greeting friends, while the

Hogarth

ENGLISH
1697 - 1764

wagon took them to Tyburn Hill, where, if they were lucky, the minister's pious exhortation and a gibbet's rope spared them from being drawn and quartered, their fragments tarred and hung on the city walls as a warning to indifferent citizens. Impressions of childhood haunt us all our lives, and Hogarth was never free of the dramatic images of cruelty so common in the society of his time.

He was born the son of one Richard Hogarth, a generation or so removed from yeoman farmers of Bampton. The father had been educated beyond the needs of a farmer, and he came to London, married, set up a school which failed, then became a hack writer. His name is still to be seen on a Latin dictionary as its author: "Ricardus Hogarth, Ludimagister." Its publisher was to make more money from another book he published at about the same time: *Robinson Crusoe*.

HOGARTH

The boy William was no student—dull classroom study could not compare to the wild life of London's streets—and soon his small, stocky figure was seen making marks on paper which he called a horse or an old biddy selling street ballads. He was apprenticed to a silver-plate engraver on Cranbourne Street, where the quality came to buy their sterling tableware, putting their money into heavy solid pieces that showed they were coming up in the world and could afford the best. So the boy with the hard, firm jaw and the high forehead bent over the gleaming surfaces of trays and pots and tea services, cutting the less important parts of armorial devices, heraldic birds and beasts, coats of arms and mottoes onto the polished surfaces.

William Hogarth learned his trade even if he didn't like it, but he spent every free moment in the streets, the taverns and the gambling halls, looking for whatever pleasure he could afford. He became a friend of the linkboys who carried their flaming torches at night to guide people being carried home by the sedan-chair men. He observed the old town walls that had survived the Great Fire, and he enjoyed the shape of Wren's new cathedral. He peered at St. James's Palace, trotted over the street stones at Westminster that still remembered the clang of the plague wagons' iron wheels and the shout "Bring out your dead!"

William already had an eye for pretty women: the drummer girls at the fair, the shrimp and orange girls who peddled their goodies in streets and theaters, the serving wenches and the bawds, the famous courtesans with black beauty patches on their white faces to accent a mouth or an eye and perhaps to hide a scar from the French pox.

Life was not only the open sewer of Ludgate, or Temple Bar with its severed limbs and skulls of traitors set up as fearful warnings. Covent Garden drew him with its singers and market shouters, Drury Lane with its theaters and gaiety. There were young bucks on the town with swords and great wigs, coming out of White's Chocolate House, having lost an estate after a night of debauchery at Mother Needham's.

All this William Hogarth felt could be captured on canvas and paper. He often stood looking up at the fresh fresco paintings of Sir James Thornhill, sergeant painter to the Crown—walls loaded with mythological trash, all awe-inspiring to a boy who also wanted to paint. But for the time being he remained the not too industrious apprentice, engraving silver jordans with a griffin per fess argent or a gules collared.

Hogarth grew into a stocky young man not much more than five feet tall, and like many short men he felt he had to prove to everyone he was as good as any man regardless of height. His manner was brisk, forward, even arrogant, and he was always ready for a fight or an insult, but quick with a laugh, a broad jest that echoed his pride in himself as a freeborn Englishman.

In 1717 he had had enough of scratching on silver and became a copper engraver, hunting out the booksellers and the publishers for illustrations to do, designing cards or letterheads. Three years later he was issuing a neat card that read "W. Hogarth, Engraver" in a design of garlands and cupids, with a well-bosomed goddess and a bearded old duffer writing something.

So we see him, a young man almost square in his truculent way, yet wearing a sword to show that he did not belong to some common trade. His first work of any value was twelve engravings for Samuel Butler's poem "Hudibras" that showed skill and energy, but no great artistic merit yet. He was taking drawing and painting lessons from his idol, Sir James Thornhill, who had a very pretty daughter named Jane whom the young man flirted with, and to whom he most likely showed his first sardonic drawings that have survived, characters done from memory at Button's Coffee House.

If Hogarth soon outgrew his master, he still attempted no great work, but took pleasure in painting small conversation pieces which showed he had a natural skill in handling oil color and a vigorous way of capturing the detail and physiognomy of London society.

HOGARTH

By now he was no longer a youth, this copper-plate hack engraver and maker of little pictures. He was thirty-one, and Jane Thornhill was twenty. They eloped in 1729 to a country cottage which Hogarth had rented, and were secretly married.

Wild, lively, happy with his new wife, now perhaps he was ready to startle London. Hogarth, as a major artist, was aware of the inexhaustible variety of life. He knew a good artist's works are a series of successful gestures—and what gestures should he make now? We have no records of anything so personal to guide us, but we know enough of his external life to sense some intangible groping for a new art form free of the old preferences and prejudgments. Hogarth disliked the dark sauces of the Old Masters' paintings; he mocked the men of taste and culture who spoke of the sacred muses as if they were ladies kept in a finishing school for young girls. The superficially jocular life of London did not fool him. He was a man marked for entanglements (unlike most modern artists he wanted no privilege of isolation) and there was enough of the Puritan past in his being to make him sense that moral solitude could end only in disaster or madness. At last he found his subject; everything was brought into unity by a single theme, and he anchored it in the stream of art with the timeless stability of his powerful shapes and his integrity as an original artist.

He set himself up as a "pictorial dramatist" and began to engrave, from a series of small paintings he had done, the copper plates of *A Harlot's Progress*. He hurried around selling subscriptions to the set of engravings. He must have been a demon salesman, for, with no reputation except as an engraver who had done some amusing little prints and pictures, this young man got 1,200 people to pay him a preliminary half guinea a piece for his history, told in pictures, of Moll Hackabout, the London demimondaine. When the plates appeared he was famous overnight. It was one of those amazing successes that come sometimes to bright young men: Lord Byron, the talk of the town with the publication of a book of poems; F. Scott Fitzgerald after *This Side of Paradise*. William Hogarth became famous and prosperous not only as an artist but as a moralist, whose lessons were preached in fashionable churches. And best of all, Sir James Thornhill forgave his now famous son-in-law for eloping with his daughter.

A Harlot's Progress still holds us. Even those not interested in art that teaches morals, not interested in pictures that tell a story, can appreciate this series as a work of art. The drawing is the work of a man

Harlots Progress Plate 1.

Wm Hogarth invt pinxt et scul.

50. HOGARTH, The Harlot's Progress: Arrival in London

Like a modern motion-picture director who claims to be a moralist while gleefully showing us the full details of sinful living, the artist, in a remarkable series of plates, follows a harlot from her start—shown here—to the grave.

Engraving, 11¾″ x 14¾″, courtesy of the Metropolitan Museum of Art, Dick Fund, 1932.

51. HOGARTH, The Harlot's Progress: Her Funeral

The harlot dead is mourned—and also picked apart—by her frightening friends. Engraving on copper, Hogarth made every detail count. The prints, which are overcrowded by today's standards, were in their day "read" like novels.

Engraving, 11¾″ x 14¾″, courtesy of the Metropolitan Museum of Art, Dick Fund, 1932.

O Vanity of Youthful Blood,
So by Misuse to poison Good!
Woman, form'd for Social Love,
Fairest Gift of Powers above,

Source of every Household Blessing,
All Charms in Innocence possessing,
But turn'd to Vice, all Plagues above,
Foe to thy Being, Foe to Love!

Guest Divine to outward Viewing,
Abler Minister of Ruin!
And Thou, no less of Gift divine,
Sweet Poison of Misused Wine!

With Freedom led to every Part,
And secret Chamber of ye Heart;
Dost Thou thy friendly Host betray,
And Shew thy riotous gang ye way,

To enter in with covert Treason,
O'erthrow the drowsy Guard of Reason,
To ransack the abandon'd Place,
And revel there with wild Excess!

Invented, Painted, Engrav'd, & Publish'd by Wm. Hogarth June ye 25 1735. according to Act of Parliment.

Plate 3

52. HOGARTH, The Rake's Progress: He Entertains

Each figure in this plate stands out fully, each is alive and busy. The rake is drunk, and the "posture woman" (the strip-teaser of the time) disrobes for her show, while a servant holds a candle and reflector to show off the act. The courtesans of the town sport and drink.

Engraving, 15⅛" x 12¼", courtesy of the Metropolitan Museum of Art, Dick Fund, 1932.

Madneſs, Thou Chaos of ẏ Brain, | With Rule diſjointed, ſhapeleſs Meaſure, | ſhapes of Pleaſure, that but ſeen | The headſtrong Courſe of youth thus run, | See Him by Thee to Ruin ſold,
What art: That Pleaſure giv'ſt, and Pain | Fill'd with Horror, fill'd with Pleaſure: | Would ſplit the ſhaking ſides of ſpleen | What Comfort from this darling Son: | And curſe thy ſelf, & curſe thy Gold.
Tyranny of Fancy's Reign: | ſhapes of Horror, that wou'd even | O Vanity of Age: here ſee | His rattling Chains with Terror hear,
Mechanic Fancy; that can build | Caſt Doubt of Mercy upon Heaven. | The Stamp of Heaven effac'd by Thee | Behold Death grappling with Deſpair:
Vaſt Labarynths, & Mazes wild.

Invented & by Wᵐ Hogarth & Publiſh'd according to Act of Parliament June yᵉ 25. 1735.

53. HOGARTH, The Rake's Progress: In Bedlam

The most famous of the artist's prints, this scene in Bedlam madhouse shows the end of the rake. He is being stripped by his jailers, while the girl he has ruined comforts him. Admission was charged to view the lunatics in Bedlam.

Engraving, 15⅛″ x 12¼″, courtesy of the Metropolitan Museum of Art, Dick Fund, 1932.

who has learned how to put the human figure and the human face together in his own way, distilling the essence of what he wants to show us and missing little of the human condition. The compositions, overcrowded, full of the juices of living and the debris of fashionable sport, high life and low, are splendidly under control. One can read each engraving like a novel, right in all its parts, yet never losing track of the central character of Moll herself. We follow the innocent country girl, seduced into her dismal trade, enjoying high life with rich protectors, spending and living at too fast a pace to survive, being arrested and sent to the Bridewell house of correction to pound hemp for the fleets that maintained English sea power. And dying in shame and disease, her very funeral turning into a maudlin gin feast.

Hogarth could not keep *A Harlot's Progress* in stock. Edition after edition was pulled, and pirate printers made their own versions of the series. There was a play, there were ballads, there were further adventures of Moll created by others. Hogarth in his bantam rage went to the House of Lords to demand legal protection for the work of engravers and artists.

He also found time for a little fun in his favorite coffeehouses and night cellars, then back to the ideas locked in his head. He never drew from life, only from memory, and each fresh print created was sold, proudly bearing the line *"W. Hogarth (ad Vivam) pinxit & sculpsit."*

Having done a woman's fall (the town wits asked, "Did she fall or was she pushed?"), Hogarth decided he would now do a series of prints on a man's world and pleasures: *A Rake's Progress.* It is the story of Tom Rakewell, man of fashion, heir to a fortune, patron of art, dissolute gambler, voluptuary, debauchee, keeper of courtesans; at last, driven mad by his excesses, Tom lands in Bedlam madhouse. No novel could compete with this pictorial drama of fashionable high life and the rewards of evil.

The series is a step up for the artist, a refinement of Hogarth's method of picturing society and the world. The compositions are still crowded (he gave the public its money's worth), but every detail is in place, nothing pushes out the roistering figure of Tom. Powerful as Hogarth's draftsmanship is, there is also monumental beauty in many of his figures and poses. Even the orgy scene with the Posture Woman undressing—a kind of primitive strip-tease—has a grandeur in its depiction of the enjoyment of the human body. There is no happy ending. The most powerful plate is fearful in its skill: Tom, driven mad, is in Bedlam, a showplace where one took one's friends and visitors to enjoy the loonies. Hogarth's age had no compassion or understanding for the lost, disordered mind. The Bedlam building was decorated with admirable statues of Melancholy and Raving Madness, and it took in four hundred pounds a year by charging a small admission fee to see the pitiable inmates.

The success of *The Rake's Progress* gave Hogarth courage to attack with stronger blows the cult of the Old Masters and the feeble, decorative painting of his time. And he kept up the production of his prints to show how art should serve society. "A Consultation of Physicians" is a mocking of the murderous quacks and sawbones of fashionable life, dangerous boobies sucking their gold-headed canes, smug under their huge tie wigs, their bloated faces greedy and ignorant. These were the popular medical murderers, with their bleedings, their cupping, the devouring mercury cures for the "French disease" (called the "English disease" in Paris), the magic baths. All the medical mumbo-jumbo, much of it still with us: the purring bedside manner, the wise, empty look, and the picking of the pockets of the ill.

A beautiful plate is "Strolling Actresses Dressing in a Barn." Here Hogarth's love of women comes forward to show us the wretchedness of backstage theater life. Yet in the young and old women dressing among the stalls and mangers of some country inn he has somehow captured the hope and beauty of people who dream of making illusion real before the footlights and reality significant. As usual, there is a great deal of detail, for, before radio, TV, fast cars, popular films, people had the leisure to approach their art with patience.

Now Hogarth issued his most mature work—a series of prints called *Marriage à la Mode*. The series was first painted, in a group of beautiful little masterpieces which have survived; these oils make Hogarth one of the grand men of paint of modern times. He transferred his story of a reckless society marriage onto copper plates with no loss of vitality. The earl and the countess, high in the court and café society of their time, marry for convenience, she to be free of her family, he for her money. Then each pursues his own idea of pleasure. Counselor Silvertongue becomes the lady's lover; he is the eternal lawyer, with the cunning fox-face that artists have been using to characterize lawyers even up to today.

As a drama the series of prints is perfect. The young married cou-

54. HOGARTH, Strolling Actresses: Dressing in a Barn

Critics think this the artist's most beautiful print. For all his dislike of the old masters, he has shown here that he could take the classical figures of high Italian art and relate them to an everyday English scene of lively, enjoyable vulgarity.

Engraving, 21″ x 16½″, courtesy of the Metropolitan Museum of Art, Dick Fund, 1932.

Marriage-A-la-Mode. (Plate II)

Invented Painted & Published by W.m Hogarth.

Engraved by B. Baron

According to Act of Parliament April 1.st 1745

55. **HOGARTH**, Marriage à la Mode: Breakfast Scene

The artist as the historian of society was never better represented than by this series on the pitfalls of a high-society marriage. Man and wife have each returned from their separate nights out on the town. The poses and gestures of the characters are among the artist's best.
Engraving, 13⅞" x 17¼", courtesy of the Metropolitan Museum of Art, Dick Fund, 1932.

Engraved by B. Baron

According to Act of Parliament · April 1st 1745

Invented Painted & Published by Wm Hogarth

Marriage A-la-Mode, (Plate III)

56.   HOGARTH, Marriage à la Mode: The Quack Doctor

The unfaithful husband has brought a young victim to a noted quack doctor for treatment.
This print is one of numerous examples from literature and art in which a satirical finger
has been pointed to the greed of certain members of the medical profession.

Engraving, 17¼″ x 13⅞″, courtesy of the Metropolitan Museum of Art, Dick Fund, 1932.

Painted by W. Hogarth. Engraved by C. Grignion.   *Published as the Act directs.*

To His Excellency S.* Charles, Hanbury Williams Embassador to the Court of RUSSIA. This Plate is most humbly Inscribd By his most Obedient humble Servant.
W.m Hogarth

57. HOGARTH, Election: Canvassing for Votes

*Only the artist has been able really to expose the eternal evil of the professional politician.
The charmer, the vote-buyer, the promiser of pie-in-the-sky, is here recorded for all time,
as he and his henchmen canvass for support.*

Engraving, 21¼" x 15¾", courtesy of the Metropolitan Museum of Art, Dick Fund, 1932.

Engraved by W. Hogarth &c. &c. &c. — To the Hon'ble S'r Edward Walpole, Knight of the BATH. — This Plate is most humbly Inscribed — By his most Obedient humble Servant

Published as the Act directs.

58. HOGARTH, Election: Voting

Except for the costumes, there is nothing out-of-date about this picture of votes being collected from the feeble-minded, the dying, the blind. In the background, England sits in a badly sprung coach while her servants gamble. All the brothers and the brothers-in-law of the successful candidate will be in public office too.

Engraving, 16½" x 20⅝", courtesy of the Metropolitan Museum of Art, gift of Sarah Lazarus, 1891.

ple yawning in the chairs of their fashionable home; each has been out all night with his own friends. The high life of the fashionable, amused by the lions of the moment—a singer, a jockey, a dancing master—and always the freeloaders, the limp-wristed hangers-on. The climax is the deadly night fight in a fashionable bagnio, where the undressed countess has been surprised with her lawyer lover, and her husband lies dying of a sword wound. Then the finale print, the scandal-filled picture of a modern marriage falling apart: her lover executed for murder, she herself dying prematurely worn out and forgotten; now there are new favorites, other dizzy vices and games.

Hogarth's indictment of a frivolous society is still potent and true. He depicted a world of pleasure that ignored the boiling up of trouble across the Channel, where soon the same sort of sporty living would result in the French Revolution and the rise of Napoleon. Hogarth seemed aware that his society was dancing near the edge of a dreadful cliff. Tory and Cockney moralist that he was, every line of his prints is a vigorous protest of society's decay. He could not be subtle like Proust, nor introverted like Kafka; neither probing the unconscious like Dostoevski nor shaping the public weal with Bernard Shaw's methods. Hogarth hit hard at both Gin Lane and Vanity Fair, and what was his reward? The very people he attacked shouted their pleasure at his droll art and bought his prints.

He lived out his life, this little man with the powerful line, making friends and many enemies, for he could not control his temper nor reason clearly in his rages. Hogarth enjoyed his life, rubbing elbows with milkmaids and orange girls, painting the wenches and servants, engraving the gamblers and the great traitors and rebels like Simon, Lord Lovat. That gross, huge man was sketched the night before his execution, counting off on his broad fingers for the artist the rebel forces he once had. "Drawn from the life and etch'd in Aquafortis."

Hogarth worked with sure skill and instinct, his pugnacious jaw jutting forward while he dreamed of a curving line of beauty. He was bewitched by the beauty of line as some men are by dreams of heaven. He read Milton, Swift and Shakespeare, or liked to give the impression he did. He knew David Garrick, the famous actor, and did a plate of him as Richard III. Hogarth strutted in his roquelaure, a many-buttoned scarlet cloak, with his pug dog Trump at his heels, until he was called Painter Pug himself. Childless, he loved animals, and owned a bullfinch which he buried with a tiny headstone:

ALAS, POOR DICK
1760
AGED ELEVEN

He did many prints, single subjects and series, the greatest of his late period being the *Election* series. In these he depicted the public swindled out of their votes by politicians, fat cats in clover—the betrayal of the right to an elected government by the Madison Avenue hucksters, the opinion makers and pollsters and party bosses of his day.

His anger and his rages, his desires and his wit, carried Hogarth along till his sudden death in 1764. In the churchyard at Chiswick his friends erected a classic urn over his grave with the words:

HOGARTH

> *If* genius *fire thee, reader, stay,*
> *If* nature *touch thee, drop a tear;*
> *If neither moves thee, turn away,*
> *For* Hogarth's *honored dust lies here . . .*
> *Here Death has closed the curious eyes*
> *That saw the manners in the face.*

To the _Right Honourable Henry Fox, &c. &c. &c._ — This Plate is humbly Inscrib'd by _his most Obedient Humble Serv.t_ W.m Hogarth

59. HOGARTH, Election: An Election Entertainment

In this remarkable composition of a Victory Gala, dozens of figures and objects are held together by the anger and skill of the artist. Now that public office has been safely delivered to the highest bidder, the faithful vote-stealers are being rewarded.

Engraving, 21¼″ x 15¾″, courtesy of the Metropolitan Museum of Art, Dick Fund, 1932.

60. HOGARTH, A Company of Undertakers, or A Consultation of Physicians

It was little more than a generation since the barber-surgeon had been more of a slaughterer than a healer. Hogarth, like most of his contemporaries, had suffered at their hands, and he showed them no mercy in these actual portraits of the A.M.A. of that time.

Engraving, 10⁵⁄₁₆″ x 7¹⁄₁₆″, courtesy Metropolitan Museum of Art, gift of Sarah Lazarus, 1891.

94

ET PLURIMA MORTIS IMAGO

The Company of Undertakers

Beareth Sable, an Urinal proper, between 12 Quack-Heads of the Second & 12 Cane Heads Or, Confultant. On a *Chief Nebulæ, Ermine, One Compleat Docter issuant, checkie sustaining in his Right Hand a Baton of the Second. On his Dexter & sinister sides two Demi-Docters, issuant of the Second, & two Cane Heads issuant of the third; The first having One Eye conchant, towards the Dexter Side of the Escocheon; the Second Faced per pale proper & Gules, Guardent. ——— With this Motto ——————— Et Plurima Mortis Imago.

* A Chief betokeneth a Senatour or Honourable Personage, borrowed from the Greeks, & is a Word signifying a Head; & as the Head is the Chief Part in a Man, so the Chief in the Escocheon should be a Reward of such only, whose High Merites have procured them Chief Place, Esteem, or Love amongst Men. Guillim.
** The bearing of Clouds in Armes (saith Upton) doth import some Excellencie.

Publish'd by W. Hogarth March the 3.d 1736

Price Six pence

It is the glory and the misery of the artist's lot to transmit a message of which he does not possess the translation.

ANDRÉ LHOTE

Piranesi

ITALIAN
1720-78

GIAMBATTISTA PIRANESI, born in Venice in 1720, was the perfectly dedicated fanatic. As a young student he tried to kill his teacher for holding back the secret of an etching acid. After five days of wild courtship he married the daughter of Prince Corsini's gardener because he was sure, by the look of her, that she was descended from the noble Romans. He once informed his doctor that his life would be forfeit if a child did not recover in a few days. When Piranesi etched his wife and their five children, they all suffered hunger and fear, not daring to move till the artist said he was satisfied with the plate.

Like most madmen Piranesi had a favorite obsession, in his case the city of Rome during a period when the entire country was decaying with poverty, cruelty and exploitation. Of Rome Piranesi made close to 1,500 huge detail-crowded and overromantic etchings, all joy to his archaeological heart. If his fame were to rest on these, he would be merely the producer of those etchings that tourists bring back from Rome. (The plates exist and are still being printed by the thousands.) Magnificent as they are in their skilled use of the etcher's needle, they are overripe, too picturesque, too much the ruins in a stage backdrop rather than the real thing. Every etching is a camera angle, each with a false scale of proportion.

It is not these works but sixteen other etchings done at the age of twenty-two that show us Piranesi as one of the great print makers. Called *Carceri d'Invenzione (Prisons)*, they are works of pure surrealist fancy. Memory becomes spherical with one-way doors; these prints are the deep probings of the madness of their creator. Space becomes huge, deep, high, in these impossible prisons of stone arches, piers and chains, bridges, stairs, ropes and trapdoors that go noplace. Here are the hells of modern man. Fantastic architectural details seem to conjure up a collaboration of Edgar Allan Poe and Frank Lloyd Wright, revealing secrets of strange, powerful dreams that no one has yet put fully into words. It is the poet of the fearful vision who is the true artist in Piranesi.

61.   PIRANESI, Prisons

The title-page picture of Piranesi's Prisons series sets a scene of chains, spikes and torture
wheels on which giants could be broken. In these etchings the artist shows that he has fully
mastered his craft—if not the dark corners of his own mind.

Etching, 21¾″ x 16⅜″, courtesy of the Metropolitan Museum of Art, Dick Fund, 1941.

62. PIRANESI, Prisons

In his handling of the forms that comprise this prison-that-never-was, Piranesi fore-
shadows abstract art, even cubism. Nothing has any meaning or goes anywhere, but forms
remain and space has an existence of its own.

Etching, 16¼″ x 21½″, courtesy of the Metropolitan Museum of Art, Dick Fund, 1941.

De Quincey in his *Confessions of an Opium Eater* writes of these prints, "Piranesi is perceived by this time standing on the very brink of the abyss."

> *Like fiend in a cloud*
> *With howling woe*
> *After night I did crowd*
> *And with night must go.*

63. PIRANESI, Prisons

The horror of the etchings in this series is that there is no horror visible. Everything is suspended in silence. The actors have departed the scene or have not yet entered. Meanwhile, everything waits.

Etching, 16¼" x 21⅞", courtesy of the Metropolitan Museum of Art, Dick Fund, 1937.

So wrote a fellow engraver, William Blake. He too imagined prisons, but he also existed on clouds. Piranesi, however, lived his secret life in dank darkness, in those prisons that inspired him when young and to which he never went back. Freud and his followers would see in this series the desire to fester in a punishing castle (Kafka's?) private and huge, where one could hiss at the world in a secret corner. They would talk of the spiny womb, the spurred flowers of steel, but this would leave our artist with only a cloudy pedigree of symbolic meanings. This world he etches is so solid, so detailed, so deceptive in its reality that one must take another track. "No irony," said Heine, "can compare with God's irony." And Piranesi seems to be predicting a kind of Orwellian horror of things to come, the pleasure domes of some rococo Big Brother. He had begun life as an architect and he was mad for stone, walls, towers, and obsessed by stairs. We can never be sure of his true meanings. A second-rate artist's qualities can be defined, but the real artist can only be experienced. Great art is a true vision among clichés, and Piranesi after these fearful glimpses goes on to his own clichés, his *Vedute di Roma* prints, playing cheerful games with the antique and baroque monuments of his city.

So we return to his prison prints, in which he tells us that all individuals are transitory objects, that awe and ideas survive anarchy only a little time. The grim joke is that his scenes here are pure anarchy, for the stairs that go nowhere, the huge instruments of torture for giants, the pulleys and ropes that seem to lift or lower nothing, are his secret writings that expressed for him, perhaps, the philosophy that we live in accordance with patterns we never fathom: from birth to death according to some secret still unexplained, and beyond all that to the slavery of time.

He may have read John Donne's *Sermons,* but it is very doubtful that he would taste or know of a heretic's prose. Yet Donne has the only true text for these strange and fearful prints:

We are all conceived in close Prison; in our Mothers' wombs, we are close Prisoners all; when we are borne, we are borne but to the liberty of the house; Prisoners still though within large walls; and then all our life is but going out to the place of Execution. . . . Now was there ever seen any man to sleep . . . between Prison and the place of Execution, does any man sleep . . . but are never thoroughly awake; but pass on with such dreams and imaginations as these . . .

64. PIRANESI, Prisons

*Lamps hang from the ceiling like sinister fruit, and two jailers appear; but they seem lost,
and they lean on each other.*
Etching, 16″ x 21½″, courtesy of the Metropolitan Museum of Art, Dick Fund, 1937.

65.   PIRANESI, Prisons

The scene here is almost festive, but when we look closer there is no clue to what is actually going on. Banners of rags, or straw? Staggering prisoners, or giants created out of old armor? We shall never know. It could be an illustration for Franz Kafka's The Castle.

Etching, 21½" x 15¾", courtesy of the Metropolitan Museum of Art, Dick Fund, 1937.

66.   PIRANESI, Prisons

The artist never explained his Prisons series. It was the work of his youth, and his later,
quite banal art never takes us into these depths of his mind or offers any key to his secret.
Etching, 21⅜″ x 16¼″, courtesy of the Metropolitan Museum of Art, Dick Fund, 1937.

Goya

SPANISH
1746-1828

To UNDERSTAND the miracle of Francisco José de Goya y Lucientes, one must know the dying world he was born into, and the modern world he helped create. The Spain of this master gilder's son, born in 1746 at Fuendetodos in Saragossa, was a nation slipping into torpor beside a dying fire. Spanish piety, based on the Roman-African agony of Saint Augustine and Saint Cyprian, was topped by royal half-wits and a court living in an outworn baroquism where Voltairean cynics played at rigid frivolities. Spain had become a kind of exotic zoo visited by Englishmen making the grand tour, or wine merchants hunting a vintage manzanilla.

The great days of *gesta Dei per Hispanos* were over, austerity and languor were fashionable, art had become a series of sacred formulas set in brown sauces with flickering red highlights. El Greco and Velázquez paintings collected smoke and tallow in darkened corners, where greasy canons droned the seven daily offices. The Inquisition still spread fear with its power to torture and roast alive. Spain having expelled its best minds and original art forms with the Jews and the Moors, life under the snow-covered Iberian sierras and in the cork forests was a dour chivalry as one waited for the holy water and the mumble of good Latin on the deathbed.

Under this crust of ritual there was modern life coming to a boil. Sparks of revolt flickered in Catalonia and Valencia, the Madrilene crowds in the Pradera de San Isidro were sharp with witty catchwords from Paris and London. On the highways, in village inns and wine shops and around the bull rings there were strong, laughing, shouting faces, faces no one painted any more: the contrabandistas, alcaldes, gypsies, *majos* and *majas*. In the sterile yellow fields the dried-out peasantry, black with sun, also waited for Goya to begin painting them.

Of Goya there is the usual story that he was discovered as a young child by the village priest, making wonderful drawings on a wall with a lump of charcoal. What is certain is that at the age of twelve he painted the altar curtain of the town church, and that two years later

P. 1

Fran.ᶜᵒ Goya y Lucientes, Pintor

67.   GOYA, Self-portrait

For all the shocking drama of his etchings, for all their detailing of cruelty of man to man, the artist chose to introduce a series of his prints with this calm, middle-class portrait of himself in side whiskers and top hat. "I can take it," his glance seems to say, "Can you?"

Etching, 8½″ x 6″, courtesy of the Metropolitan Museum of Art, gift of Mrs. Francis Ormond, 1950.

a rich patron, impressed with his work, sent him to Saragossa, the capitol of Aragon, to train as an artist. We know little of his art studies at the studio of José Luzán, where he copied prints, but there are many stories of his café brawling, running with the wild crowd of matadors and *aficionados* in the bullfighting set, singing and dancing the bolero at the many fiestas. At nineteen he is supposed to have been involved in some underworld killing and to have been hunted by the Holy Office.

He turned up at Madrid, still wild and still fascinated, according to the stories about him, by the semiunderworld of the *corridas;* but again there are no actual documents to prove he got a knife in his back and was smuggled to the coast by a band of bullfighters and put on a ship for Italy. All we do know is that by 1771 Goya was in Rome. He collected Piranesi's famous etchings of prisons and ruins, and again there are stories (with no proof) that he enjoyed the carnivals of the courtesans and bandit life, climbed the huge dome of St. Peter's to carve his name on the great lantern, and broke into a nunnery and tried to carry off a girl. He was the kind of a young man whom people tell strong tales about.

Back in Spain, he did banal ecclesiastical church art; he had little belief in a formal, organized godhead. At twenty-nine he married the sister of the court painter Bayeu. He kept his wife perpetually pregnant, and of their huge progeny (she bore the artist twenty children) only one rather dull son reached maturity. Goya was not a faithful husband and he continued to live his own life, still attracted to the world of bullfighters and gypsy girls. His brother-in-law got him into court circles.

In his youth Goya was of the party of Sancho Panza, not that of Don Quixote. He accepted and took part in the concupiscence of court life, used Iberian lethargy as a platform to his own success. He had a huge appetite for everything under the blue-tiled Moorish towers. Goya was a needy provincial out to conquer a city and a court, and if adultery was an easy step to success, he did not hesitate. It would take age and illness and deafness to turn his vision inward. Young and ardent now, he bowed with the rest at the monstrously snobbish court, accepted baroque opulence and painted the gold and lace with an agile line. Only a few saw how at times he mocked royal features, how hollow were his holy pictures.

He tried to cultivate *gracia y simpatía,* warmed his hands politely

68. GOYA, Caprichos

Like all artists, Goya was interested in the contrast between the beautiful and the ugly, between youth and old age. Here a brooding old hag watches a young girl add to her charms.

Etching, 8½" x 5¹⁵⁄₁₆", courtesy of the Metropolitan Museum of Art, gift of Walter E. Sachs, 1916.

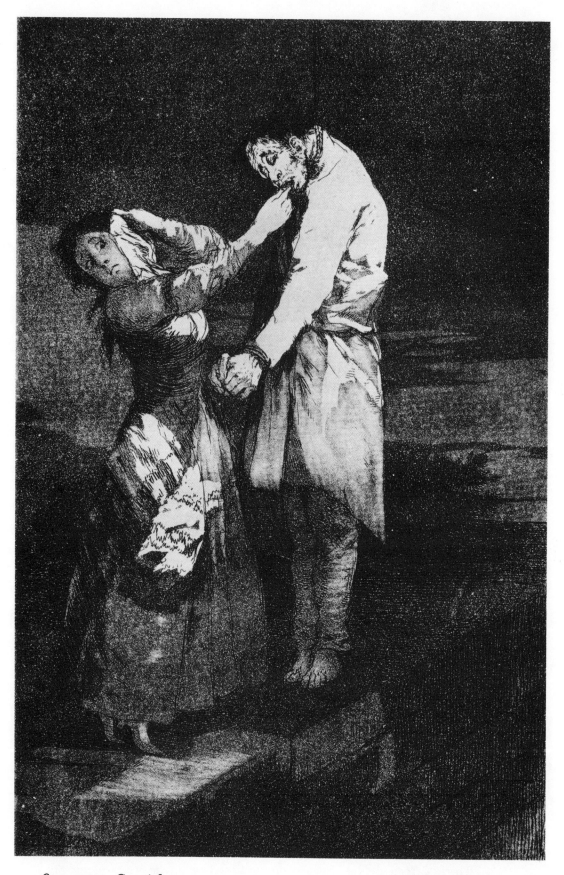

69. GOYA, Caprichos

The touch of a hanged man was supposed to have magical qualities. The woman's pose shows how the power of superstition can drive people to perform any frightening deed.

Etching, 8⁷⁄₁₆″ x 5⁷⁄₈″, courtesy of the Metropolitan Museum of Art, gift of Walter E. Sachs, 1916.

over a fire of charcoal and olive stones, drank the proffered glass of manzanilla wine a patron offered, stood in doorways at palace balls listening to the pizzicato of fiddles and stored up the follies of this society for his later work.

Goya painted portraits of himself at all stages of his life, so we can see him, bull-necked, skeptical, a man of appetites. His face was solid, but not the face of a peasant; rather, it had the square features of a tradesman's son, from a family trying to better itself. When he was making a great deal of money he lived like a peasant and collected no art treasures. He overate like a starved mule, and in his thirties his iron constitution already was shattered by Spanish cooking and wild living.

He was commissioned to do a series for the royal tapestry factory, thirty designs. He created Spanish genre subjects: pelota players, alfresco diners on the grass, freaks, markets, lovers. They are gay, light, beautiful. At forty he was president of the Royal Academy of Fine Arts and was named one of the King's painters. If he had died at forty, the name Goya would mean little today. He had painted some skillful pictures, he had designed some charming tapestries. But the real artist, the true creative frenzy in him, was yet to emerge.

On the death of his father, he locked himself into a room, refused food (always a sign of trouble with this heavy feeder) and began to etch dozens of copper plates, mostly memories or copies of work by other artists. A year or so later he nearly died of indigestion, and in his self-portraits he looks like a dissipated, prematurely old man. To this period belongs his affair with the Duchess of Alba, whom he is supposed to have painted as "The Maja Naked" and "The Maja Dressed." *Maja* can be translated as "noble lady and harlot," and this seems to be a good description of the woman. Goya was carried away, almost to madness, with his passion for the dark, slender vixen. The affair became a court scandal and the Duchess retired to her estate in Andalusia. Goya followed and caught a chill, and eventually total deafness set in. Other accounts say he had the first attack of his strange illness in Cádiz. It left him dizzy and partly blind, with a buzzing in the head; for a time his right side was paralyzed. He recovered but was partially deaf and in a state of sullen despair.

The Duchess, surrounded by other men, drove him to etch her as a two-faced woman: "The Dream of Lies and Inconstancy." Between his deafness and a sudden plunge into emotional tragedy, his vision cleared till he saw a full picture of his world and the true condition of

GOYA

Spain. He began in his sickness to etch the famous plates for his series called *Caprichos de Goya.*

Goya was now obsessed by man's helplessness in the grip of inexorable circumstances, and the seeming indifference of the universe. It was the artist's duty to project man's capacity to be almost infinite. Yet Goya in his dark moments felt only an empty negation and an awareness that the essential nature of things will never be fully revealed. He had turned to pleasure till it failed him. "Every Spaniard," said Ganivet, "carries a passport saying, 'This man is entitled to do whatever comes into his head.'" Goya had carried several such passports in his *cordobán* hat.

GOYA

He saw, as he etched, that we topple from one extreme to the other, hurry from the active to the contemplative life, as if changing horses or lovers or clothing will get us off the ground. He was to create a great plate: A family sits in the branch of a huge tree, alone, huddled together, children, parents, grandparents. The horizon is blank. The great branch creaks in a silent wind. Here for the moment is safety and warmth. Goya seems to say that elsewhere social expediency has long since defeated transcendental morality, has boiled down courage, hope and sacrifice to polite phrases available to all. Only in the family, together in the tree, is there a moment of tranquillity before the storm.

Goya did not buy ready-made beliefs by the pack; he rolled his own ideas. And while they might not be as neat as those philosophies stamped out in standard sizes, they tasted better to him because they had for him a home-grown honesty.

When he shows himself in the *Caprichos* dressed in a top hat, his thick neck in fashionable stock, looking prosperous and satisfied, we have only to turn to the other prints to know this is a brave pose. The artist is well aware that every day is Judgment Day and that we dress for it as we pull up our boots. He began more and more in his etchings to try to communicate what is incommunicable.

The *Caprichos* prints are social commentary, in which Goya mingled the *Walpurgisnacht* world of his imagination with stark reality, the inner vision with the outer landscape. He anticipated Freud in the print "The Dream That Produces Monsters." He is much taken with the ideas of love and women, and their influence on fashion and pleasure in the world. The writer Gautier says of these prints, "One of his sketches consisting of four touches of his graver in a cloud of aquatint tells you more about the manners of the country than the

Aguarda que te unten

70. GOYA, Caprichos

Witchcraft in the artist's day was not taken lightly or as an old wives' tale. Most Spaniards believed then that devilish creatures such as these existed in the real world and close at hand. "Wait for them to dip you," the caption reads.

Etching, 8½″ x 5⅞″, courtesy of the Metropolitan Museum of Art, gift of M. Knoedler and Co., 1918.

71. GOYA, Caprichos

A majestic use of black and white that captures the mood of brooding Spaniards, the twist of a man's leg, the coyly covered heads of the girls. Gallant as the subject is, there is no hint of any pleasure in the print; "Poor girls!" the caption reads.

Etching, 8½" x 5⅞", courtesy of the Metropolitan Museum of Art, gift of M. Knoedler and Co., 1918.

Asta su Abuelo.

72. GOYA, Caprichos

A fine modern use of the etcher's needle and of the acid wash that controls the grain of the background. The subject is someone proud of his family tree—jack-asses all, "even to his grandfather," as the caption says.

Etching, 8½″ x 5⅞″, courtesy of the Metropolitan Museum of Art, gift of M. Knoedler and Co., 1918.

73. GOYA, Caprichos

Bad deeds must be punished, and as soon after the deed as one could catch the culprit. A broken pot is being paid for here, in a heroic composition worthy of a more noble subject.

Etching, 8½″ x 5⅞″, courtesy of the Metropolitan Museum of Art, Dick Fund, 1930.

74.   GOYA, Caprichos

The love of the dead shown here suggests more than a man who has broken into a tomb to mourn his beloved. Spain itself, the artist may be saying, is partly a corpse, looking only to a dead past.

Etching, 8 1/16″ x 5 7/8″, courtesy Metropolitan Museum of Art, gift of Walter E. Sachs, 1916.

longest description." It is a full world he gives us: monks eating, young girls showing their special charms, old hags selling virtue, stuffed officials being barbered for the pompous dullness of their lives; lovers, soldiers, peasants, soothsayers, all busy at their little rounds that make up a world.

Naturally the Inquisition moved in on the *Caprichos* as being heretic. The King took over the plates to save Goya from the Church's torture cells. Yet Charles IV was a true Bourbon, trying to live like the *ancien régime* (he was a dead shot at rabbits), while Queen Maria Louisa looked like a broom-riding witch and kept a stable of human studs. Goya painted this pair with all their children, and the result is a glowing satire. One critic called the picture "the grocer's family who have just won the big lottery prize."

GOYA

The Duchess of Alba, worn out with her rage for life, died in 1802. Goya's wife died in 1804. Deaf and ill, Goya was left with a weakling son and the horrors of the wars against the French. He painted the street fighting, the dreadful executions of civilians (how mild they now appear compared to the scientific murder of millions by the Germans in their gas furnaces). And Goya etched the series of prints *Los Desastres de la Guerra* (*The Disasters of War*). No artist before or since has pictured so perfectly the madness and futility of human warfare. Against bare, broken landscapes he pictured war in every brutal aspect. They are among the greatest prints ever engraved on copper.

By 1818 Goya was stone deaf, and he bought a house outside Madrid, Quinta del Sordo, the house of the deaf man. Here he painted the silent walls with his dark pictures—*pinturas negras*—that by their style presage the impressionists of the nineteenth century and the expressionism of the twentieth. Saturn devouring his children, the congress of witches presided over by great male goats, all done with slashing lines and dark, loaded brushes. He also experimented with the first lithograph plates, returning to his fascination with contests between men and bulls, the *faena* with cape, the final *suerte*.

War came again and a reactionary government made him accept exile. He went to Paris, then to Bordeaux, where he did his greatest bullfight prints. He was seventy-eight. His philosophy of *Nada*, nothing, was behind him. Now he wanted only to work, locked away from all sound, away from his native soil. Working, Goya lived, and working Goya died, in April 1828, at the age of eighty-two.

75. GOYA, Pedro Romeno

To Goya, the bullfight was not the intellectualized "moment of truth" that Anglo-Saxon writers have described. Here he is composing in space, and the blank areas of the print are as important to the picture as the man and the bull.

Etching, 12¼" x 16⅜", courtesy of the Metropolitan Museum of Art, Rogers Fund, 1921.

Today his ashes are in the Church of San Antonio de la Florida in Madrid, under his beautiful, gay murals which reaffirm that among much darkness there is sunshine and laughter. And that people taking their pleasures as they find them are all living under sealed orders, while the artist lights matches to warm and make visible a corner of the universe.

76. GOYA, Spanish Pastime

Turning from etching to the new art of the lithograph, Goya mastered it at once. Here again, it is not the ritual or the art of bullfighting that interests him, but the vision of men and beasts in senseless sport.

Lithograph, 12¼" x 16⅜", courtesy of the Metropolitan Museum of Art, Rogers Fund, 1920.

77.   GOYA, Brave Bull

The artist does not take sides. Only the eyes of the fallen horse show an awareness of the horror. The rest are too intent on the contest. The bullfighter impaled on a horn seems almost relaxed now that the worst has happened.

Lithograph, 12¼″ x 16⅜″, courtesy of the Metropolitan Museum of Art, Rogers Fund, 1920.

78. GOYA, Divided Arena

This great print is an amazing work of art for any period; but it breaks with the calm, formal compositions of the artist's time and shows us the common people at their uninhibited pleasures.

Lithograph, 11¹¹⁄₁₆" x 16⅜", courtesy of the Metropolitan Museum of Art, Rogers Fund, 1920.

79. GOYA, The Proverbs

Of all his mysterious prints, this is the strangest: a family, isolated, living in a tree. Here is a basic unit of society, banded together in the void of life's enigmas.

Aquatint, 14¹⁄₁₆″ x 18¹⁄₈″, courtesy of the Metropolitan Museum of Art, Dick Fund, 1924.

Por qué?

80. GOYA, Disasters of War

No other artist of his time dared to show the true horror of war. To the others it was all brave men in fine uniforms seated on good horses and shouting for victory. Goya turned away from that masquerade to produce an unsurpassed series of etchings on the evil and stupidity of men fighting men. "Why?" the caption asks pointedly.

Etching, 5⅜″ x 7½″, courtesy of the Metropolitan Museum of Art, Schiff Fund, 1922.

Grande hazaña! Con muertos!

81. GOYA, Disasters of War

What a beautiful machine is the human body, the artist is saying, and how cruelly this machine treats its fellow machines. Even the tree, burdened with its grim fruit, seems to struggle in agony. "A great feat! With corpses!" is Goya's bitterly ironic caption.

Etching, 5⅜″ x 7½″, courtesy of the Metropolitan Museum of Art, Schiff Fund, 1922.

Tampoco.

82.   GOYA, Disasters of War

The sheer horror of this series often causes one to overlook the very skilled use of the etcher's needle. Here it has delineated a sparse landscape in which everything has been pushed aside to catch the fearful drama of the one moment that tells everything.

Etching, 5⅜″ x 7½″, courtesy of the Metropolitan Museum of Art, Schiff Fund, 1922.

Las resultas.

83.   GOYA, Disasters of War

Men are cruel enough to each other on a physical level, but Goya was also aware of the forces that feed on disaster and of the harm war can do to the human mind. Here is the horror of war in terms of a nightmare that is half real, half fantasy.

Etching, 5⅜″ x 7½″, courtesy of the Metropolitan Museum of Art, Schiff Fund, 1922.

84. GOYA, Caprichos

Alone in his studio, the artist has fallen into a troubled sleep over his work, and the monstrous thoughts he kept from his mind in his waking hours now come to hover. But his cat is not frightened; its strange, cruel eyes have seen the worst.

Aquatint with etching, 8½″ x 6″, courtesy of the Metropolitan Museum of Art, gift of M. Knoedler and Co., 1918.

IF WILLIAM HOGARTH is the artist as stern moralist, Thomas Rowlandson is certainly the artist as cheerful rake. He caught the flavor of an age with his gay, sardonic pen and the etching needle; his huge *oeuvre* is aesthetics geared to a laughing indignation, but never to mere moralizing. During his lifetime George III would be crowned and would fumble away the American colonies; there would be the French Revolution, the Gordon riots, the rise and fall of Napoleon. Rowlandson the artist would have something to say about the men and women who were the actors in many of these events.

He was born of a merchant family in 1756, in the section of London called Old Jewry. The boy grew up pampered by his family, loved by his aunts and uncles, walking the London streets. The last city walls were removed in 1760, letting the modern world into a town busy making money, attending cockfights, showing off its styles at the Ascot races, the bloods and bucks giving a knee to their battered champion at the matches of the bare-knuckled pugilists. Over it all hung the yellow-gray smoke of sea coal burning in Georgian fireplaces.

Thomas Rowlandson was boarded at the school of the Reverend Cuthbert Barwis, A.M., at the Soho Academy, where he was already drawing skillfully at an early age, expressing his admiration for fine living and good fun on the margins of his schoolbooks. At fourteen he entered the Royal Academy School at Somerset House, where his delight in drawing from the nude did not prevent his potting the models with a pea shooter. From sixteen to eighteen he is supposed to have been sent by a rich aunt to a school in Paris, where—in addition to becoming a boulevardier and spending much time at the gambling tables—he studied works of *outré* caricature and Continental draftsmanship and line, and visited the Bibliothèque Nationale, admiring and copying the work of Rubens, Boucher's pink meat-pie nudes, Teniers' and Isaac van Ostade's pictures of Dutch low life and horseplay, and Callot's slim, elegant French lines.

Rowlandson

ENGLISH
1756-1827

Modern research says no to this once-accepted period in his life: the rich aunt is a myth, the two years in Paris were at the most six weeks. Yes or no, he was referred to at the Royal Academy as a "bloody Frenchman" and he spoke the French language well.

His entire reputation as an artist of importance is based on his drawings, water colors and prints, yet he began his artistic life by setting himself up as a portrait painter in oils. Only two of his oil paintings have survived, although Rowlandson's early work once hung with Romney, Gainsborough and Moreland. But he is at his best in his drawings of popular social scenes, his "stained drawings" (as water colors were then called). He eventually turned away from salon oils, and by 1784 he had begun to outline the faces of the streets and the passing parade of high and low life. A friend of the period chided him on his "misfortune of possessing too ready an invention," adding, however, that some of his subjects were "so replete with a painter-like feeling that Sir Joshua Reynolds and Sir Benjamin West pronounced them wonders of art."

He also devoted himself to gambling and late hours, and there are a great many stories of his adventures on the town with Jack Banister, the actor son of an actor father, and Henry Angelo, whose father was the royal fencing master. Yet he also found time for a great deal of hard work. Often he would be at the gambling table all night and all the next day, stopping just to gulp some food and drink, and then, a heavy loser, would hold up his pencil and say, "Here is my magic wand. I'll find my success with it." His work was already in the private collection of the young rakehell Prince of Wales (later George IV) at Windsor Castle, where it was kept under lock and key; and it was described in British understatement as "notoriously of a free tendency regarding subject."

Rowlandson loved life. He was a huge, powerful figure of a man with a portly bearing (he admired his paunch), and the Roman face of a minor Caesar. He was already aware of the pecking order of society and, like Thackeray later on, was to record his own image of a social order that would dance at a ball the night before Waterloo. Meanwhile, he etched ten plates he called *Anatomy Diversions,* later collected as "Pretty Little Games for Young Ladies and Gentlemen . . . by T. Rowlandson. A few copies only printed for the artist's friends."

85. ROWLANDSON, The Sculptor Nollekens and His Venus
The sculptor Nollekens helped fill Westminster Abbey with banal and graceful works. This print is a satire on the reproduction of classical art by men who were insensitive, as Rowlandson was not, to the wonder of living flesh.
Etching, hand-colored, 11¼" x 8⅝", courtesy Metropolitan Museum of Art, Whittelsey Fund, 1959.

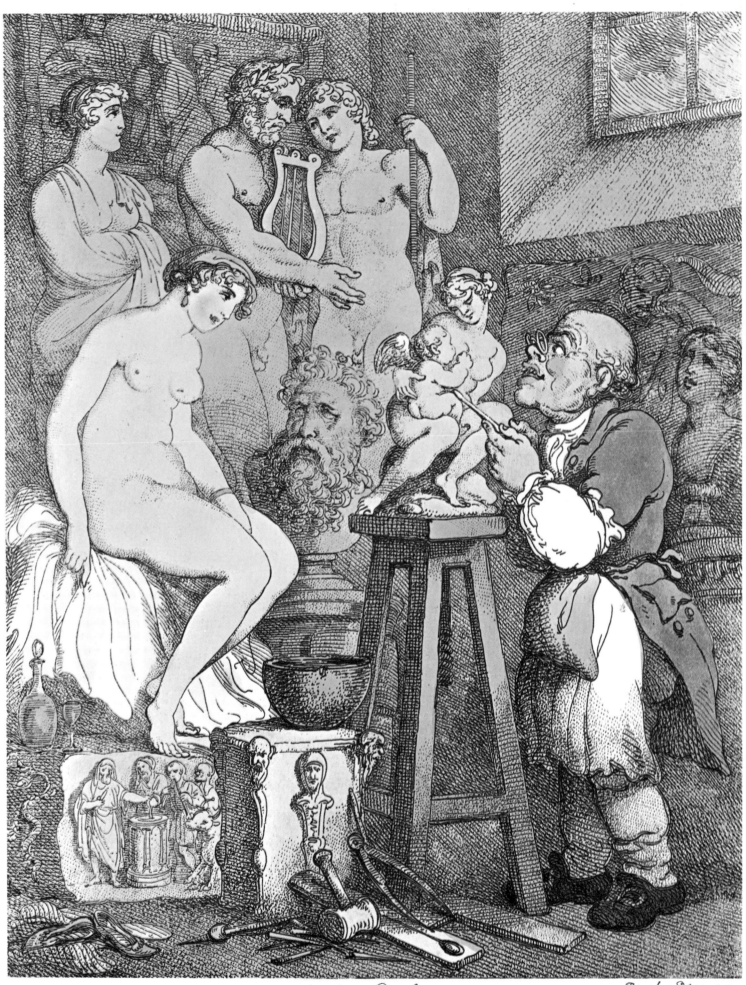

The Sculptor

Rowlandson inv.

129

Pub. Jan.1.1807 by R.Ackermann. — Repository of Arts 101.Strand

MISERIES of SOCIAL LIFE.   7 Dialogue

Sitting for hours before a smoky Chimney, like a Hottentot in a craal — then just as your suffer-
ings seem at last to be at an end — puff, puff — whiff whiff. again far more furious than ever — add
to this a scolding Wife?—

Rowlandson del et sculp.

87. ROWLANDSON, Grog on Board

A direct statement is made and a solid pattern is created with a few scratched lines and some simple tones. The woman is most likely Rowlandson's lifelong companion, Betsy Winter.

Etching, hand-colored, 14½″ x 18¾″, courtesy of the Metropolitan Museum of Art, Whittelsey Fund, 1959.

86. ROWLANDSON, Careless Attention

The power of unity in this plate is amazing. Its parts are briefly sketched, yet subject and humor are fully captured. The artist brings us right into his drama and neither points a finger nor draws a moral.

Etching, hand-colored, 12¾″ x 15⅞″, courtesy of the Metropolitan Museum of Art, Whittelsey Fund, 1959.

88. ROWLANDSON, Miseries of Social Life

Rowlandson's etchings on copper differ from all engravings done before him in that they are composed of the outlines that people and objects take on in an atmosphere of smoke and color. Everything is suggested; nothing is finished in detail.

Etching, hand-colored, 4⅜″ x 6¾″, courtesy of the Metropolitan Museum of Art, Whittelsey Fund, 1959.

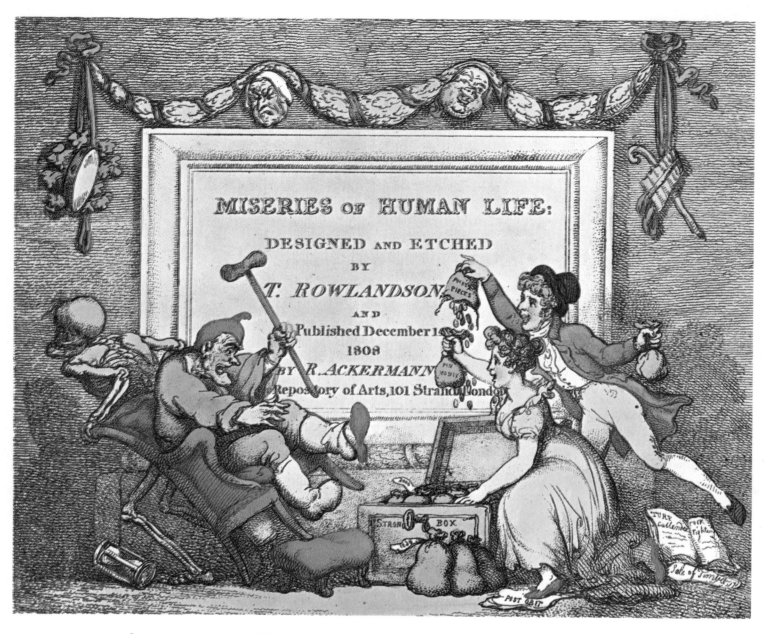

89.   ROWLANDSON, Miseries of Human Life, Title Page

Rowlandson's love of life and its good things is here extended even to a title page. To him, life was short and old age no pleasure. The color in his etchings was added by other hands and only suggests the great beauty of his water-color paintings.

Etching, hand-colored, 6¾″ x 10″, courtesy Metropolitan Museum of Art, Whittelsey Fund, 1959.

He was amused to observe the fast life around him—the bears at fairs dancing to pipe and tabor, the balls in fine wainscotted assembly rooms lighted by candles in silver sconces, the trips to bathe at Harrogate, Scarborough and Epsom, where the supercilious and dandified, the gouty, the forgers and the highwaymen sported. Rowlandson's work began to take on a sharper, more sardonic edge; if these were the best people, protected by the Royal Navy and trade treaties, life was an amazing charade.

He drew the fat old men with their great lower jaws, their paunches and gouty legs, swallowing their ox cheek and burgundy, claret and partridges. He drew the masked ladies, lightly dressed, going to meet lovers in sedan chairs hired at three miles a shilling. And always the artist drew the three-bottle parsons in queue and gaiters, who were fine on horseback in a society fox hunt ("the unspeakable after the uneatable," someone said). He pictured John Bull as an apoplectic-faced country squire riding the rough roads in his gilded carriage, with shaggy postilions whipping up the horses. Horses and dogs Rowlandson loved almost better than people; cats he hated and feared.

It was a world of wit, grace and genius, too; he bowed to Brummell and Chesterfield across the gaming tables and watched Horace Walpole swish by, enjoying the sight of running doormen in scarlet livery. He watched the beaux at their chocolate and the jack-booted cavaliers from the Horse Grenadiers and the Life Guards eying lovely women. He sported with the rest while recording it all on copper plates. Thus he became not a well-tailored Jeremiah crying in the wilderness of St. James's Park, "Vanity, vanity, all is vanity," but, rather, a not-too-innocent bystander.

It took a strong man to live in two worlds, as Rowlandson did—the fashionable Hanoverian society and the world of the hard-working artist in his flat in the Pantheon on Poland Street, and later on St. James Street, Adelphia. At times he was even a publisher, and some plates read "Designed and published by T. Rowlandson." But he usually worked for the famous print publishers: Ackerman's Repository of Art on the Strand, Tegg of Cheapside, and Mrs. H. Humphrey, who also published Rowlandson's only rival of real merit, James Gillray.

Artists got no royalties in his day; a plate was sold outright for from two to five pounds on the average. So Rowlandson was always hunting for new subject matter—*bon vivants* and milkmaids, roisterers and hay harvesters at their play, pox doctors and doxies. In politics

ROWLANDSON

INTRUSION ON STUDY OR THE PAINTER DISTURBED.

90. ROWLANDSON, Painter Disturbed

In this print, a simple comic situation is handled with brilliance of form and movement. The beauty of the model, the distress of the surprised painter and the amusement of the uninvited guests have been caught perfectly.

Etching, 10″ x 13⅞″, courtesy of the Metropolitan Museum of Art, Whittelsey Fund, 1959.

he was nonpartisan (he delighted in drawing the dainty duchess kissing the fat, greasy butcher for a vote). He was a city man, but he loved the country. He traveled on the Continent and to Wales and Cornwall, and he drew the rustic humor under thatched huts, drew the inns, the tinkers' markets, the seaports full of sailors, fishermen, brawling fishwives and fluttering skirts on windy days.

He thrived nicely, and there was a brisk demand for his engravings. His plates were quickly done, quickly printed and speedily colored and sold in the shops. They are not the careful work of Hogarth, nor is the detail laid on like an inventory of a shop's contents. Rowlandson's work has the grace of an artist who puts in only what is needed. His people rush to play or parade, strut, make love, with the pleasure of well-drawn bodies aware that man's time on earth is short. Morals are for Sundays in church and don't belong in inked lines skillfully applied.

There are hints in the details of his work that he hid true sensibilities under a gay aplomb. He was a hedonist who was aware of the thinness of the worldly wisdom he carried as a banner. We see a need to hurry; everything moves quickly in his art—the wind, the horses, the sea—as if there were only a little time left. Life is something that you create in time and store in art, a collection of impressions to be hunted down, nailed and transformed into intellectual essences called music, art, literature. If not, they are gone forever, he seems to hint. The artist is a gravedigger, an opener of tombs—he overcomes death and returns things to life. Art was a religion for Rowlandson; it endowed human endeavor with the truth which a few minds refine. But it's not easy to be so immersed in eternity, and Rowlandson refused to think too much.

At his best his prints are hymns to living fully; in his ironic moments they are the texts of the materialist's message: "This is a world I never made, but it's the only world we shall ever know." And then there are the dark, coarse plates with that smell of the gibbet, the doss house, the great London sewers, the festering alleys. They were done at a time when the public was accustomed to realistic books, like those of Smollett and Fielding, and no one objected to the true picture of things. These prints we may find too strong for our own hygienic times, when life is cleaner but perhaps duller.

Rowlandson's own life was far from dull. He was knocked down one midnight on Poland Street and his watch and money were lifted.

ROWLANDSON

There were rumors that he was married, but at his home there was only a very pretty housekeeper, Miss Betsy Winter, to greet him when, past fifty, he went dragging a rheumatic leg up the stairs, getting a little dizzy with the climb. He mocked marriage for the artist in a famous plate, "The Chamber of Genius," where the poor wretched artist is living in poverty with a lie-abed wife, two soiled children, and a cat and a dog fighting and upsetting pots – the artist in debt, struggling to turn out the hack work that supports his dismal ménage.

He was coming to know the other side of the shield of pleasure. He did a series of prints on the luxuries and miseries of human life, showing the hard lot of the poor, the sailor, the soldier, the street beggar. Napoleon was on the march, the nation of shopkeepers was threatened, and Rowlandson attacked, in lusty plates, this "upstart Corsican, the Bloody Boney."

Then, like Daumier, he found his own version of Don Quixote in a bony, lantern-jawed, pedantic old parson called Dr. Syntax. Rowlandson created him and saw him mocked, tossed and cheated at every turn. The good old parson inspired some of the best plates Rowlandson did. They appeared first in *The Poetical Magazine,* and a hack poet named William Combe, while locked away in debtors' jail, did the text, rhyming and satirizing to fit the prints. They were collected in three volumes: *Dr. Syntax in Search of the Picturesque, Dr. Syntax in Search of Consolation* and *Dr. Syntax in Search of a Wife.* It is a grand tour of England, from London to the beautiful Lake District, to the cathedral towns, the inns and byways – a splendid picture of an age and a people. He did a similar coverage of England's capital in his series *Microcosm of London,* 104 aquatint plates, with the architectural draftsman Augustus Charles Pugin doing the background of churches and buildings—a brilliant collaboration.

Aging and ill, Rowlandson thought much of death and turned his mocking line on it. In a macabre moment he looked at Holbein's famous *Dance of Death,* those prints that point to the futility of human endeavors and pleasures. Again Combe whipped up a passable text, and Rowlandson did his own English *Dance of Death,* in many ways his most beautiful print series. A yea-sayer still, he followed it with *The Dance of Life.*

What he had to say of life and death he said with no fear. He still went to the Bell and to the Coach and Horses. But he was worried that his vogue was passing. Younger men were appearing on the scene. He threw himself harder at his copper and aqua fortis, swinging the etch-

ROWLANDSON

92. ROWLANDSON, Miseries of Social Life: Dining

He loved dogs, hated cats and was a victim himself of the flowing bowl. The howling, gorging, blustering sportsmen he depicts here also provided inspiration for Dickens and other writers, who re-created this world in prose.

Etching, hand-colored, 4⅜" x 6¾", courtesy Metropolitan Museum of Art, Whittelsey Fund, 1959.

MISERIES DOMESTIC.

Waking in the middle of the night, in a state of raging thirst eagerly blundering in the dark to the washing stand, and there finding the broad mouthed pitcher which you lift to your lips, so full that besides amply satisfying your thirst, it keeps cooling your heated body, and purifying your linen with the overplus.

91.   ROWLANDSON, Miseries, Domestic

Rowlandson was a free-living rake, and to him all domestic scenes were misery. Such was his skill with a pen that a few curved lines could bring a figure into breathing life—even if, as in this case, he did not wish to flatter.

Etching, hand-colored, 5⅜″ x 7¼″, courtesy Metropolitan Museum of Art, Whittelsey Fund, 1959.

Pub. Jan 1, 1807 by R. Ackermann. —   — Repository of Arts 101 Strand

MISERIES of SOCIAL LIFE. . 7 Dialogue

Dining, and passing the whole evening with a party of foxhunters, after they have had what they call "glorious sport", and while you execrate the very name of a hound, being gorged with the crambe recocta of one chase after another, till you wish the country was under ground."

Rowlandson delet sculp.

CORDIALS.

T. SLANO

POLITO

SPORTS OF A COUNTRY FAIR *Part the Second*

93. ROWLANDSON, Sports of a Country Fair

The print began as folk art, crude and often vulgar. Here Rowlandson depicts the common sports of the common people, with all of his subject matter intact and undoctored. He is not looking down at their play but joining them.

Etching, 9⅛″ x 13⅛″, courtesy of the Metropolitan Museum of Art, Dick Fund, 1917.

ing needle, the burnisher, the roulettes and burins of his trade. He had gambled away fortunes; now he began to wonder whether poverty or death would win the close race to the end. The great feasts of the past, the Homeric drinking, the debauches of youth and middle age were demanding payment from his big body. The world was changing, too. If he lived too long there would be prim Queen Victoria who was to sweep the lusty side of society under the rug.

When Rowlandson died in 1827 he left the house and some money

THE LAST JIG OR ADIEU TO OLD ENGLAND.

94. ROWLANDSON, The Last Jig!

This is not folk art. The drawing is too sharp and original, the figures and faces are rendered too knowledgeably to be anything but the creations of a great artist using the scenes of his times as a starting point. These seamen about to ship out are as lively and fun-loving as any sailors of today.

Etching, 8½" x 12⅞", courtesy of the Metropolitan Museum of Art, Dick Fund, 1917.

to "Miss Betsy Winter, Spinster of West Wycomb, now residing with me." He was buried in St. Paul's Churchyard, Covent Garden. It was written of him, "He has covered with never flagging pencil enough to placard the whole wall of China, and etched as much copper as would sheathe the British Navy." He was not an artist given to futile introspection, but one must always think of his work in the light of his famous print "Time and Death Outwitted by the Historian and the Painter."

95. ROWLANDSON, Amputation

Mankind has suffered much at the hands of the medical profession. The faces here shown are actual portraits of local sawbones, and the scene is not too great an exaggeration of eighteenth-century reality.

Etching, hand-colored, 11″ x 14½″, courtesy Metropolitan Museum of Art, Whittelsey Fund, 1959.

THERE WAS ONE who heard no gay street peddlers singing, "Fine Seville oranges, inside and rind! Ripe peacods, sixpence a peck!"

The most tragic of the great print makers of Regency England was James Gillray. He, rather than Hogarth or Rowlandson, is the true father of modern political cartooning and caricature; without him men like Low and Herblock today, and the first American pioneer, Thomas Nast, might have been without method or symbols. Gillray invented many of the stock figures of international events and incidents still in use. His English, German, French and Russian characters that symbolize those nations are still common coin and have, of course, become banal and hackneyed by their constant reappearances in modern time. But Gillray was more than a remarkable political commentator; he was an artist of dazzling draftsmanship. Certain of his copper engravings have a delicate quality and economy of line that make them stand up with the best of any artist, though a great deal of his work and that of his contemporaries is too strong for us, belonging to a hardier age and a tougher appraisal of life. It may well be not the times that are out of joint, but ourselves.

James Gillray, the son of a one-armed Scottish soldier who settled in England, was born in London in 1757. His father was the sexton of the Moravian burying ground at Chelsea for forty years. We know little of the son's childhood, but it appears to have been an unhappy one and to have set the pattern for Gillray's deranged life, for the manic-depressive state in which he spent most of his adult years. Early he was apprenticed to the engraving trade and, like Hogarth, worked on silver and engraved cards. Bored, he ran off with a band of strolling players and suffered greatly in damp and dirty country inns and drafty halls, and from the mocking he most likely received from the players and their raucous company. Then, disillusioned by stage life, he returned to London and enrolled in the Royal Academy School of Art, where the careful detail and skill of his early work soon attracted attention.

In 1779 he issued to the trade the first print we know of, "Paddy On Horseback," a satire on the wild Irish character, here riding a bull

Gillray

ENGLISH
1757-1815

96.   GILLRAY, The Morning After Marriage

Gillray's skill as an etcher has never been shown to better advantage than in this tender satire on a runaway marriage—in this case, of Mrs. Fitzherbert and the Prince of Wales, who could not marry publicly because she was a Catholic and a commoner. The setting, the three beautifully drawn people, all bring the past to life and into immediate focus.

Etching, 16¼″ x 33″, courtesy of the Metropolitan Museum of Art, gift of Mrs. Marshall P. Slade, 1940.

A VOLUPTUARY *under the horrors of Digestion.*

97. GILLRAY, A Voluptuary

What other artist has captured with such skill the pleasures of the flesh—and their out-come? Here George IV, as Prince of Wales, is etched by the greatest needle of his day in a striking vision of sensual gluttony.

Etching, 16¼″ x 11½″, courtesy of the Metropolitan Museum of Art, gift of Mrs. Marshall P. Slade, 1940.

A COGNOCENTI contemplating y̆ Beauties of y̆ Antique.

98.   GILLRAY, A Cognoscente

The art snob, the avant-garde *phony and the greedy dealer are not phenomena of our time alone. Here a notorious eighteenth-century collector views art of the past which was again in fashion then—and consisted mostly of fakes.*

Etching, 14″ x 10″, courtesy of the Metropolitan Museum of Art, gift of Mrs. Marshall P. Slade, 1940.

backward. He was soon a popular print maker and his work much in demand. Gillray was a magnificent engraver; neither Hogarth, with his heavy line and overcrowded detail nor Rowlandson, with his hasty needle and indifference to background, could approach the skill with which Gillray engraved and etched copper in various styles. His more ponderous and overdetailed plates are no longer fashionable, but others, delicately etched plates with the busy charm of his brisk line, the scribble of his darting forms, show much taste and wit.

He worked directly on the copper plate, creating his prints without any previous drawing of the theme, referring only to some small cards with sketches of heads for possible use. His entire production is so large and varied that one wonders how this imprudent man, intemperate, often sunk into dementia, could produce such vital and firmly drawn prints, and so many of them.

For many years he lived in the house of his publisher, Mrs. Humphrey of St. James Street. As one polite Victorian historian puts it, "It has been whispered that there was a liaison between Gillray and Mrs. Humphrey not essential to their relation as designer and publisher; it is due to the memory of the lady to contradict that slander." We shall leave it at that.

The pick of his prints (best in their uncolored state) are "The March on the Bank," a lively mocking of official dignity; "Frying Sprats" and "Toasting Muffins," two small masterpieces showing the parsimonious George III and his Queen at breakfast; "The Cow Pock," a reactionary attack on Jenner's new inoculations, which were to make the world safe from smallpox; and "The Morning after the Marriage," a beautiful, sensual plate about a royal honeymoon. His many graphic attacks on Napoleon enraged the subject greatly. Usually his plates are found heavily colored for sale in the shops, which is a pity, as much of the artist's remarkable skill in etching is thereby lost. Gillray alone of his generation's famous artists experimented with the new art of lithography—grease drawing on stone; he did one plate, and also several woodcuts.

He worked diligently, but his life was darkened by heavy drinking and by periods of black despair. Often when he craved alcohol and had exhausted his fees from Mrs. Humphrey, he would work secretly for other publishers under different names, and even in other styles. In 1811, during a fit of despair and delirium, he threw himself from an upper window of the house on St. James Street. He survived, but for the remaining four years of his life he did little work; he is buried in the churchyard of St. James's, Piccadilly.

Dr. Johnson once remarked of drunkards, "He who makes a beast of himself gets rid of the pain of being a man." Gillray never succeeded in getting rid of the pain. Yet this sick, unhappy man opened up new vistas for artist-historians and gave the world a fresh language of images and symbols to explain passing events and the people who make them.

The Cow Pock — or — the Wonderful Effects of the New Inoculation! — Vide. the Publications of ye Anti-Vaccine Society.

99. GILLRAY, The Cow Pock

Like Bernard Shaw, the artist had little faith in the medical profession. Smallpox inoculations have saved millions of lives, yet to the people of Gillray's time the idea of being injected with cattle pox was regarded with a mixture of fear and amusement.

Etching, 9⅞″ x 13¾″, courtesy of the Metropolitan Museum of Art, gift of Mrs. Marshall P. Slade, 1940.

The PIC-NIC ORCHESTRA

100. GILLRAY, The Pic-Nic Orchestra

Gillray was a folk artist. He had no high-flown theories or ideals of art. What he observed of life he re-created on his plates as satire, often so successfully that we forget to note the skill with which he drew.

Etching, 10⅛″ x 13¾″, courtesy of the Metropolitan Museum of Art, gift of Mrs. Marshall P. Slade, 1940.

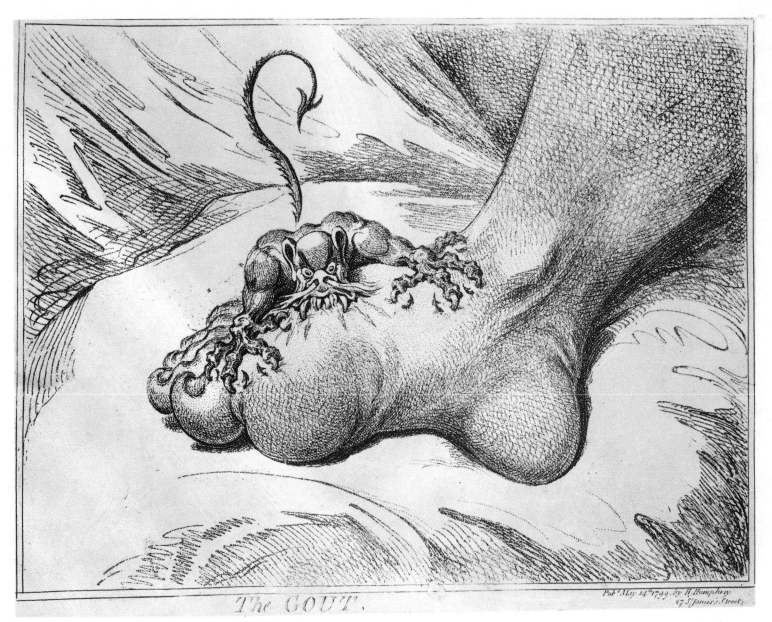

The GOUT.

*Pub.ᵈ May 14ᵗʰ 1799 by H. Humphrey
27 S.ᵗ James's Street*

101. GILLRAY, The Gout

The artist was not afraid to depict frightening or ugly aspects of life. He and his friends did not work for museums, critics or dealers, but for the common people, who had no fear of confronting life's realities as re-created through the artist's imagination.

Etching, 10½″ x 14″, courtesy of the Metropolitan Museum of Art, gift of Mrs. Marshall P. Slade, 1940.

DIDO FORSAKEN. *Sic transit gloria Reginæ*.

Pub.d May 21.st 1787. by. S.W.Fores. Piccadilly. London.

102. GILLRAY, Dido Forsaken

The Prince of Wales had secretly married Mrs. Fitzherbert, a commoner and a Catholic, but, as the price of having his huge debts settled by Parliament, he allowed the marriage to be repudiated. The Prince is being carried away by three statesmen—Fox, Lord North and Burke—while Pitt and Dundas are blowing from Mrs. Fitzherbert's head the coronet of the Princess of Wales and the crown of a future Queen. Mrs. Fitzherbert is prepared to follow the example of Virgil's Dido when deserted by the faithless Aeneas. In cartooning this sensation of his day, Gillray created a memorable etching of a female figure.

Etching, 10⅞″ x 14¾″, courtesy of the Metropolitan Museum of Art, gift of Mrs. Marshall P. Slade, 1940.

A MARCH to the BANK. Vide *The Strand, FleetStreet, Cheapside &c. Morning & Evening.*

103.   GILLRAY, A March to the Bank

In 1787 the Gordon Riots in London almost brought on a civil war. In the midst of violence and chaos, a special effort was dedicated to saving the Bank of England. This masterly plate shows the government callously trampling on human misery to protect Albion's gold.

Etching, 16¼" x 33", courtesy of the Metropolitan Museum of Art, gift of Mrs. Marshall P. Slade, 1940.

London. Pub.d Nov.r 26.th 1791. by H. Humphrey N.o 18. Old Bond Street

FRYING SPRATS.

Vide. Royal Supper.

104. GILLRAY, Frying Sprats

London, Pub^d Novr 28th 1791. by H. Humphrey, N:18 Old Bond Street

TOASTING MUFFINS.

Vide. Royal Breakfast.

105. GILLRAY, Toasting Muffins

*"Frying Sprats" and "Toasting Muffins" are a matched set of plates
mocking King George III and Queen Charlotte. The royal pair lived
with an unroyal frugality, and although their homely domesticity
was a subject of derision in court circles it eventually proved a
source of popularity with the people.*

Etchings, both 7⅝" x 5¾", courtesy of the Metropolitan Museum of Art,
gift of Mrs. Marshall P. Slade, 1940.

To see the world in a grain of sand,
And a heaven in a wildflower;
Hold infinity in the palm of your hand,
And eternity in an hour.

Blake

ENGLISH
1757 - 1827

No ONE EVER EXPRESSED better the art and the ideas of William Blake than he does here in his *Auguries of Innocence*. Poet, engraver, philosopher, inventor, printer, publisher, nudist, more than slightly mad at times, and often too sane for this world, Blake, a delirious symbolist and visionary, has puzzled some and given much pleasure to many. Let us, his best work seems to say, forget practical great men—all they ever do is mislead the world.

He was born in 1757, in London; his father was a hosier and a Swedenborgian mystic. The mystic son followed, part way, in his father's footsteps. In the England of royal beef-red George, where Hogarth and Rowlandson enjoyed the gross pleasures, the world of rat fights and Tyburn hangings, Blake grew up with only a toe touching the London sidewalks, their coffeehouses, gambling halls, bagnios and royal horseplay. At four he clearly saw God peering in at him through the window. Later he found a nest of angels in congress up a tree, and he plainly talked to Ezekiel out of the Old Testament (in a field) and was soundly whipped by his mother for the tale. All his life Blake lived in London's pea-soup fog, yet visited with spirits from outer space. He escaped Bedlam, but not a touch of divine madness.

The boy began to draw early, and he served seven years of hard, dull apprenticing in the engraving trade with a man called Basire. Blake made himself a master engraver and later invented a relief etching process which is not fully understood even today.

At twenty-five he married a market gardener's illiterate daughter, who signed the marriage certificate with an X. The husband taught her to read, write, color his drawings, and walk thirty miles at a stretch into the country when the mood was on him. Except for three years among the green fields at Felpham, where he got into trouble, all of Blake's life was lived in London.

He believed firmly that he was divinely inspired, and he and Mrs. Blake proved they were Adam and Eve, open to temptation, by sitting naked in their back garden. He lived poorly in this world as a commer-

106. BLAKE, Book of Job: When the Morning Stars Sang Together

The most beautiful and touching of the Job prints. The group of angels is related, with poignant joy, to the outspread arms of God. This is exquisite lyricism.

Engraving, 8⅛″ x 6½″, courtesy of the National Gallery of Art, Rosenwald Collection.

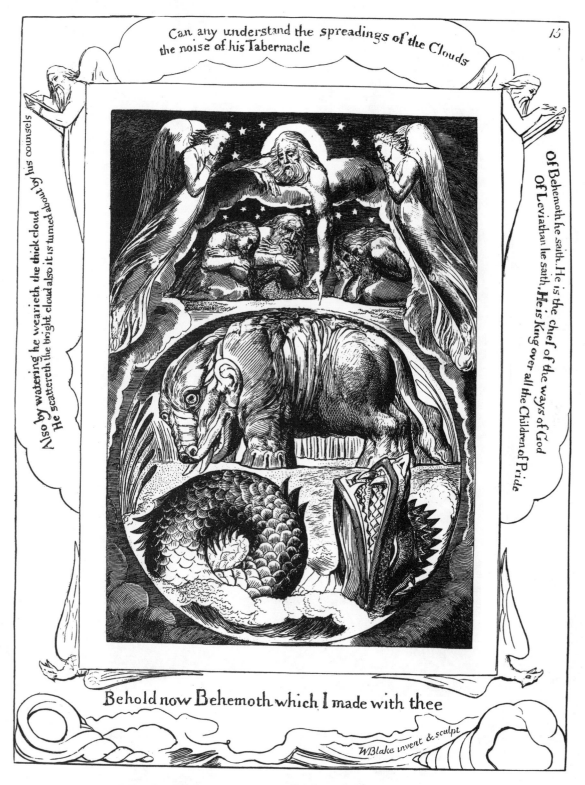

Within the illustration:

Can any understand the spreadings of the Clouds the noise of his Tabernacle

Also by watering he wearieth the thick cloud he scattereth the bright cloud also it is turned about by his counsels

Of Behemoth he saith. He is the chief of the ways of God Of Leviathan he saith, He is King over all the Children of Pride

Behold now Behemoth which I made with thee

WBlake invent & sculpt

107. BLAKE, Book of Job: Behemoth and Leviathan

Blake's engravings for the Book of Job stand among his greatest works. He had no fore-father in English art, and his Old Testament world is the most personal version of it until we come to Chagall.

Engraving, 7⅛″ x 6″, courtesy of the National Gallery of Art, Rosenwald Collection.

108.   BLAKE, Book of Job: There Were Not Found Women Fair
       as the Daughters of Job

The artist fills space in his own way. The pattern is one of abstract units, and the figures, the action, must be fitted into it. Images are transposed; heaven becomes earth and man becomes God with great ease.

Engraving, 7⅞″ x 5²⁹⁄₃₂″, courtesy of the National Gallery of Art, Rosenwald Collection.

cial engraver and spent the free part of his time writing, designing, engraving and coloring his own neglected books. He decorated a half-dozen unreadable epics and twenty tragedies and illustrated the Book of Job (perhaps his most magnificent prints) and the works of Milton, Gray, Cowper and others. As a poet, he is one of the glories of English literature.

> *I give you the end of a golden string;*
> *Only wind it into a ball,—*
> *It will lead you in at Heaven's gate*
> *Built in Jerusalem's wall.*

BLAKE

"I should be sorry if I had earthly fame," he said. "I wish to do nothing for profit. I wish to live for art. I am quite happy." He lived often on only ten shillings a week in a two-room flat. A simple, gentle man with a true love of humanity, yet given to fits of temper against salon art and fancy artists, he would sit drinking his beer brought home from the local pub and working over his mystic plates and often more mystic texts. Blake was an unconventional artist, with an overlighted lucidity, a crystalline imagination that was often stuffed with theosophical rubbish. Yet at other times he was breathtaking, his opaque mind pulsing to unseen drums. The enigma of his envelopment in transcendentalism is part of his art, for his work is hallucination given form. Realistic art Blake called "the blot and blur method of imitation . . . the fool often does it best, as it is the work of no mind."

He used his inflammable imagination to create prints of audacious abstractions. Inspiration, he felt, is the only true revelation. Man is an organism trying to act like a machine. "Nature is the work of the Devil . . . reason is the dull, the dead, the natural." He spurred his imagination to catch at visions; he once showed an angel's feather he had picked up on the ground. A solitary, Blake felt the whole world was out of step.

Looking at his best prints, one is struck by the slimness of the basic material he worked with. He drew from a stirring cosmography of God and angels in passage to Paradise, all based on the engravings he had seen of Michelangelo, Raphael and other Italians, copies of Gothic tombs in Westminster Abbey, and models Blake took over from his friend Henry Fuseli, a Swiss artist of erotic content but skilled craftsmanship. Fiends, angels, rocks, stars, and muscles never found in practical anatomy all dance for Blake in illimitable ecstasies, and will

109. BLAKE, Dante's Inferno: The Malebranche Tormenting Ciampolo

The engraving in this series is superb, the style monumental. We are held with hypnotic intensity by this picture of demons tormenting a mortal. The drama is conveyed by a theatrical use of well-drawn legs, probably copied from Michelangelo.
Engraving, 9⅜" x 13¼", courtesy of the National Gallery of Art, gift of W. G. Russell Allen.

for us if we let them. His images are symbolized by familiar actors in his cosmic dreams, all vividly embodied; they are presences he just saved from banality by his humorless intensity. We don't dare laugh, and soon we are touched by the innocence of what he called "my spiritual models in the flat world of the imagination." He washed luminous color over his prints, and we ignore, in their brilliance, the deficiencies of the detail in the drawing.

The precision of Blake's conceptions overcome all his meager equipment. He had a mind not anchored too firmly to this earth, but he was no charlatan weaving meaningless eccentricities. He truly

110.   BLAKE, Dante's Inferno: The Whirlwind of Lovers

The sins of the flesh have never been so well depicted as in this picture of doomed lovers flowing along in a spiral of clinging bodies. In every possible and impossible position they spin by into time and memory.

Engraving, 9½″ x 13¼″, courtesy of the National Gallery of Art, gift of W. G. Russell Allen.

III.   BLAKE, Dante's Inferno: The Circle of the Falsifiers

The epic style of the Italian poet merges with that of the Englishman in these plates illustrating the Inferno. Blake has re-created the huge myth in a landscape we shall not see again until we come to the surrealists.

Engraving, 9½″ x 13⅜″, courtesy of the National Gallery of Art, gift of W. G. Russell Allen.

Leaning against the pillars. & his disease rose from his skirts
Upon the Precipice he stood: ready to fall into Non-Entity.
Los was all astonishment & terror: he trembled sitting on the Stone
of London: but the interiors of Albions fibres & nerves were hidden
From Los: astonishd he beheld only the petrified surfaces:
And saw his Furnaces in ruins, for Los is the Demon of the Furnaces:
He saw also the Four Points of Albion reversd inwards
He siezd his Hammer & Tongs, his iron Poker & his Bellows.
Upon the valleys of Middlesex, Shouting loud for aid Divine.

In stern defiance came from Albions bosom Hand, Hyle, Koban,
Gwantok, Peachy, Brereton, Slaid, Hutton, Skofeld, Kock, Kotope
Bowen, Albions Sons: they bore him a golden couch into the porch
And on the Couch reposd his limbs, trembling from the bloody field.
Rearing their Druid Patriarchal rocky Temples around his limbs.
All things begin & end, in Albions Ancient Druid Rocky Shore.)

112. BLAKE, Jerusalem: "... Leaning against the pillars."

Blake's own process of relief etching is revealed here. Instead of the customary procedure of using acids to bite an impression into the copper, he employed them to eat away the unwanted parts of the plate. The result is as bold as a woodcut.

Relief etching, 8⅞″ x 6½″, courtesy of the Library of Congress, Rosenwald Collection.

113. BLAKE, America: Frontispiece

Regardless of size, Blake's pictures always have scale. His figures—nude, often winged—are sensuous yet cerebral. They brood with a certainty of purpose, trying to relate us to an unseen world beyond material reality. America, A Prophecy *was a poem written by the artist and published in 1793.*

Relief etching, 9¼″ x 6¾″, courtesy of the Library of Congress, Rosenwald Collection.

gives us his own frenzy as we look at the flowing friezes of bodies in his prints for Dante's *Inferno* and the Book of Job—the rhythmic sweep of man and woman, of sky and landscape. His angels and demons in their fervor and wrath, scorn and supplication, give our age of unbelief a glimpse of what once was impressive to earnest minds.

Blake worked and lived and died almost unknown except to a few friends. In 1827 he was indifferently buried with three poorhouse paupers in an unmarked grave.

> *And did those feet in ancient time*
>   *Walk upon England's mountain green?*
> *And was the holy Lamb of God*
>   *On England's pleasant pastures seen?*

BLAKE

A hundred volumes of his manuscript texts and drawings were burned after his death as inventions of the Devil. But his surviving works have the qualifications to survive a tempestuous eternity. The Philistines and the Pharisees now collect William Blake. He has proven that when reality walls us in our spirits cut an opening to freedom.

As a later, also tormented artist, James Joyce, put it:

There is a certain resemblance between the mystery of the Mass and what I am trying to do. I am trying to give people some kind of intellectual pleasure or spiritual enjoyment by converting the bread of everyday life into something that has a permanent artistic life of its own for their mental, moral and spiritual uplift.

Illustration from *Gates of Paradise,* courtesy Library of Congress, Rosenwald Collection.

OF ALL THE GREAT woodcut artists, the closest to us–the one Westerners understand best–is Katsushika Hokusai. He was a restless, unpredictable man; he lived in close to a hundred different houses and changed his name at least thirty times. Here clearly is the pattern of a complicated spirit that would require a Dostoevski or a Faulkner to do it justice. He is neither shy nor retiring; he hides in no silken tower playing the pure artist. He was un-Japanese in his loudness, his boisterous manner, his brash ability to attract attention. For a very great artist, he acted at times like P. T. Barnum or a Hollywood producer peddling trash. He had a restless, titanic dissatisfaction with the accepted viewpoint, a curiosity and a drive for novelty that children usually outgrow.

Hokusai

JAPANESE
1760 - 1849

Hokusai was born in 1760 outside the city of Edo, in the Katsushika district of the province of Shimofusa. He always delighted in calling himself a peasant. Actually he was apprenticed early in life to a mirror maker for the shogun and then worked in a lending library, where he was fascinated by the woodcut illustrations of the piled-up books. At eighteen he became a pupil of Katsukawa Shunsho, the great artist of actor prints. Hokusai was soon signing himself Shunro, and for the next fifteen years he too made actor prints and also illustrations for popular novels. By 1795 he was calling himself Sori and had been infected by the European copper etchings which were slipping into the country. Perspective, shading, the striving for reality, all gripped him for a while. Every time he changed his name he changed his style. He painted, he designed fine *surimino* (greeting prints), he boldly attacked pure landscape. With Hiroshige he created the modern Japanese landscape school. He did famous views and began making prints of *The Station of the Tokaido Road* twenty years before Hiroshige did his own series.

Hokusai never stayed long with a period. Always he was off and running to something new. A great show-off, he painted with his fingers, toothpicks, a bottle, an eggshell; he worked lefthanded, from the

114.   HOKUSAI, A Folk Hero

Some of the best of Hokusai's prints are in black and white. This one and the next four are from a book about a popular hero. The refinement of cutting is amazing.

7⁷⁄₁₆″ x 10⁹⁄₁₆″, from the author's collection.

115.   HOKUSAI, A Battle

Fallen rider, fallen horse, all is confusion. This is not to be seen at a glance, but read almost like a page of text; soon everything falls into place.

7½″ x 10⁹⁄₁₆″, from the author's collection.

116. HOKUSAI, A Duel

In this print the artist resorts to pure pattern. The woodcut is a fine balancing of blacks, solid as night, against lines as thin as a hair.

7⁷⁄₁₆″ x 10⅗⁄₁₆″, from the author's collection.

bottom up and from left to right. Once he painted two sparrows on a grain of rice. Commissioned by a shogun to decorate a door of the Temple of Dempo-ji, he tore it off its hinges, laid it in the temple courtyard and painted blue wavy lines on it to represent running water; then he dipped the feet of a live rooster into red seal ink and chased the bird over the painted door. "Your Highness, see the River Tatsuta in autumn," he said, bowing when the shogun came to view the finished job. The shogun and his retinue saw at once the river and the falling red maple leaves of autumn. Another time Hokusai used a large broom dipped into a vat of ink to draw the full-length figure of a god, over a hundred feet long, on the floor of a courtyard. He was an intrepid egoist, who was also capable of integrating experiences into permanent forms.

At the age of fifty-four, Hokusai began to issue books of his sketches which he called *The Manga*. These give marvelous glimpses into the mind of an artist who found nothing not worth sketching; radish grinders, horse gelders, pancake women, street processions, jugglers, wrestlers—all went into his sketchbooks. It was then that he produced his great series *Thirty-six Views of Fuji,* a remarkable set of woodcut prints that tell the story of the countryside around Edo: people at play or work, great waves engulfing fishermen, silks drying in the sun, lightning playing on great mountain cones, and always, somewhere, the sacred ash-tipped top of Fuji. He was a tremendous artist with a unique awareness, daring anything, creating a new type of figure, the little grinning Japanese citizen who bears his burdens, is amused at life, goes his way—a Japanese Everyman. He also illustrated the plays of the kabuki theater and the sacred legends, filling volumes with pictures marked by his powerful line, his ability to depict fights and lovers and landscape with a furious skill that seems effortless, yet is so full of knowledge and love. He loved to draw ghosts. How dead are the dead, he asks, if they walk in our dreams?

He did thirty thousand pictures during a full and long life. And when he was an old man he recorded his hope of holding back disintegration long enough to touch immortality:

From the age of six I had a mania for drawing the shapes of things. When I was fifty I had published a universe of designs. But all I have done before the age of seventy is not worth bothering with. At seventy-five I learned something of the pattern of nature, of animals, of plants, of trees, birds, fish and insects. When I am eighty you will see real prog-

HOKUSAI

169

117.   HOKUSAI, Farm Life

Nothing escapes the all-seeing eye of Hokusai. His animated little figures carry on their daily tasks graced by the artist's love for them. He was, indeed, as he once signed himself, "Old-Man-Mad-About-Drawing."

7³⁄₁₆″ x 9⅞″, from the author's collection.

118. HOKUSAI, Crossing Stream

From overripe heroics to the simple grace of everyday scenes such as this, the artist demonstrates his wide range. Nothing could be more direct and placid than the print above.

7⅛″ x 9⅞″, from the author's collection.

ress. At ninety I shall have cut my way deeply into the mystery of life itself. At a hundred I shall be a marvelous artist. At a hundred and ten everything I create, a dot, a line, will jump to life as never before. To all of you who are going to live as long as I do, I promise to keep my word. I am writing this in my old age. I used to call myself Hokusai, but today I sign myself The-Old-Man-Mad-about-Drawing.

He didn't reach a hundred and ten, but he nearly reached ninety. On the day of his death, in 1849, he was cheerfully at work on a drawing. He faced his end with amusement, as his last letter to a friend shows:

HOKUSAI

The King of the Infernal Regions is old and retiring from business and has built himself a pretty house in the country. He's asked me to come and paint a picture for him. So I'm leaving, and I'm going to take my drawings with me. I'm going to rent a studio at the corner of Hell Street. I'll be happy to see you any time you're passing by.

119. HOKUSAI, Scene from a Legend

A fox turned into a woman caused the hero to commit strange deeds, of which this is one. The artist succeeds in suggesting landscape, facial features, costumes and weather by his masterful combinations of line.

15″ x 9⅞″, from the author's collection.

120.   HOKUSAI, The 47 Ronin

This is the great kabuki drama of outlawed warriors who avenge their dead master and then kill themselves. Here a few of them have found the villain in a chest.

9½" x 14⅝", from the author's collection.

見附 附つけ 見み

東海道
五十三次
二十五

121. HOKUSAI, On the Tokaido Road

The artist did series after series of scenes and events on this famous road and its way stations. A notorious prankster, Hokusai has here placed his publisher's seal (Iri) on the horse's rump.

9⅛" x 6⅞", from the author's collection.

122.   HOKUSAI, A Moon Bridge

Most of Hokusai's prints are highly detailed, but he could also dispense with detail and still capture the full values of his subject. All is suggestion in this picture.

9¾" x 15", from the author's collection.

177

123. HOKUSAI, Lake View

One of the artist's most beautiful prints, this calm landscape is very unlike his usual work with its crowded and impassioned style. The bars of mist are a convention for showing the often rainy weather of Japan.

9¹⁄₁₆″ x 6¾″, from the author's collection.

124. SHARAKU, Actor in Female Part

Women were not permitted to appear on the Japanese stage. All female parts were played by actors who usually specialized in such roles. Sharaku's prints, which at first appear to be cartoons, are actually deep character studies.

14½″ x 9¾″, from the author's collection.

125. SHARAKU, Actor Playing a Money Lender

The artist is able to get behind the elaborate make-up and even the tradition of playing certain emotions with crossed eyes, to reveal to us the personality of the actor.
14⁷⁄₁₆″ x 9½″, from the author's collection.

AT THE END of the eighteenth century the country of Japan was ruled by the Tokugawa shoguns—meaning "barbarian-destroying generals"—and their shouting swordsmen, while the Mikado, a descendant of the sun itself, held no power and lived with some placid, fan-waving nobles in Kyoto. There were five kinds of people in the land: the lords, the samurai warriors, the farmers, the craftsmen and a new class arising with vulgar cheerfulness, the traders and merchants. There was order after a dreadful epoch of warring, a cruel but reasonable justice. The real rulers were the shoguns with their military or *bakufu* government threatening all with the cutting edge of steel; they kept the Emperor as a harmless symbol to command the loyalty of the common people.

There was no contact with the outside world but for some Dutch traders restricted to a small island, and all foreign influence was repelled with violence. So the samurai and their leaders sat contented, unaware that the wealth of the land was slowly passing into the hands of the traders and merchants—and with it a growing desire for pleasure and comfort. Artists and actors were beginning to mock slyly, with expressionless faces, the iron-armored strutters with their two swords and ribbon-tied topknots.

In the early days of their power, the first Tokugawa shogun went to the empty lands of the east coast, to a reedy marsh where there were no hills, only the wild grass and a hundred-hut village called Edo. Ignoring the ancient traditional cities such as Kamakura, he built his new capitol there. Great moats were dug and a stone castle was built behind them. And by the time the Yasukuni Shrine, the business district of Nihombashi, the grand park at Ueno, the shops, theaters and jugglers of Asakusa and, beyond the city, the gay dissolute streets of the walled Yoshiwara were added, Edo (later called Tokyo) was a great city of a million and a half people. Pleasure, art and business were Edo's reasons for existence, and the country people said, "A true citizen of Edo never keeps a coin in his pocket overnight."

To capture this time and its pleasures, certain schools of painters

Sharaku

JAPANESE
C. 1794

SHARAKU

began to utilize the woodcut print at the end of the seventeenth century. It was called the *ukiyoye,* which can be translated (rather poorly) as "pictures of the fleeting world": the world of pleasure, of the courtesans and the packed theaters where the kabuki actors performed. The latter, on their part, were producing a vigorous, almost vulgar art, not unlike the melodramas of our early Western films. Unlike European artists until recent times, the Japanese—using water colors or a brush dipped in a rich, freshly made black ink—worked quickly to capture the emotion or shape of the moment, the gestures and poses of the fleeting scene. They preached no sermon, offered no message or moral except one of pleasure and color: the beauty of a darting curve, the grace of balanced flowing pattern that brings to flower in the beholder's mind a sensitivity and a welcome to full living. They pictured the beauty of women, the grace of dancers, the movements of crab-armored men in battle, the ceremonies both large and small that added up to perfectly mannered attitudes. It was a ritualistic and beautiful way of life floating on a dogma of obedience and cruelty—a culture that believed one must caress the favorites, avoid the unfortunates and trust only the gods. There was no idea of being true to nature in this art, of brooding on great moral themes, or illustrating a historical event in a pompous, humorless manner. Of the artists who worked in this popular print field, who toiled for small pay for the publishers and the print sellers, there is very little recorded. They were considered mere worthy craftsmen, like lantern makers, roof builders, umbrella menders—artisans who added to a way of life but were never the equal of lords or samurai.

Among the great artists of Japan, the one called Toshusai Sharaku is the most elusive. He is like someone glimpsed down a crowded street of Edo, perhaps a thin young man dressed in a *nō-gaku* dancer's robes, shy, even unsocial, avoiding one's look, and then he is gone, swallowed up in the milling crowd around the theater posters. He may be seen at the *sumo* matches of the giant wrestlers, or escaping from a teahouse when the fumes of sake fill the small square room as the guests sit listening to a geisha reciting. In the end one gives up trying to create an image of Sharaku; the mystery will never be revealed, the artist captured, portrayed or questioned.

In 1794, for something like three hundred days, we know his prints were being cut, printed and sold. Toshusai Sharaku was the name he used in this period; that we are sure of, for it was signed to his color prints. Then, failing to find a public, Sharaku is gone again, and we never catch another glimpse of him in Japanese art or history. All that is left are a few facts, some legends, a lot of hindsight guessing, *and* over one hundred bold and splendid colored woodcuts. His prints shocked their time and were ignored, yet they extended the field of the ukiyoye with a broad sweep. They are now so rare that wealthy collectors hoard them as precious possessions.

Sharaku's is the banal story of a great innovator being neglected in his time by the critics and art lovers, whose eyes are usually open only just far enough to see what is fashionable at the moment. Almost all of the best woodcut artists of the period found no merit in Sharaku, this young man with his large heads of popular actors in their best or most notorious roles, all drawn with a mocking directness that seemed to many little better than the cartoons children draw on walls.

The great artist Utamaro, a drunkard genius whose tall and stately women are one of the glories of the print art, said of the actor prints that Sharaku was designing, "They are portraits showing the least attractive of human traits." In a book called *Ukiyoye Ruiko*, a study of the print art, there was written of Sharaku's work: "These pictures of kabuki actors are badly drawn in an attempt to exaggerate reality, and they will be of no enduring interest to the world of art. In a year or so they will have no importance at all." And one Shikitei Sambo, a writer, merely records, "He lived at Hatchobori, in Edo, and worked for only half a year."

The rest is silence, at least for seventy-five years. Then, in 1868, while the surviving prints were still considered to have no value, a writer named Tatsuta Shashukin added a few new items of information on the artist's life. Where he got them, how true they are, we do not know. He states baldly that Sharaku's true name was Saito Jurobei, that he lived in the section of Edo called Hatchobori, and that he was a *nō-gaku* actor in the company of Hatchisuka Haruteru, thirteenth Lord of Awa. The figure of the artist grows a little clearer; we see him in the suite of a great lord, one of a company of actors and dancers performing the stately rituals of the prescribed drama, so different from the popular and wild kabuki theater. Yet it may all be fiction, imagined by a harassed writer filling a book a publisher demanded on the popular arts. Or it may be the truth. To the Japanese it mattered little. Few cared about or had even heard of an obscure print maker named Sharaku who had lived four or five generations before.

Meanwhile Japanese prints had gone abroad, and they greatly influenced the impressionist painters in Paris and Whistler in England and delighted certain collectors on the Continent. That most of the prints were the later vulgar works of Kunisada and his followers, with their glaring bad color and frenzied, overviolent postures, didn't matter. The newness, the directness, the novel compositions of the Japanese art form had caught the eyes of the European artists set on destroying the stilted salon painting of Paris. Sharaku was not one of the gods of the Paris studios or galleries. It was Hokusai and Hiroshige — later artists — who were lifted high in the esteem of the French critics and boldly acclaimed as the greatest practitioners of the art of ukiyoye by men who had never seen the glory and power of early artists like Masanobu, Toyonobu, Kiyomitsu, Harunobu *or* Sharaku.

SHARAKU

Not till 1910 did Sharaku begin to come into his own. It was then that the German critic Julius Kurth published his book *Sharaku*, demanding for his hero a high position in the world of art, on a level with Rembrandt and Velázquez. It was a bold, arrogant declaration and perhaps overstated the case. Kurth added little to the few known facts about the artist Sharaku; he stated flatly that the artist had matured and grown up as a *nō* actor under the crest of Lord Hatchisuka, in the province ruled by the proud Awa clan.

Kurth's book did create a demand for the prints of this newly discovered genius. The Japanese themselves by this time were aware that most of the great prints of their color-block artists had slipped away from them, out of the country. They began to study the case of Sharaku. Now the merry-go-round of conflicting experts began to spin, throwing off new discoveries and new facts, few of them true. In 1925 it was claimed by a Dr. Ryuzo Torii that he had discovered the actual tombstone and epitaph of Sharaku, and that his true name was really Haruto Jizaemon, a *nō* actor of the Haruto school. Later a newspaper in Tokushima claimed to have found records in Toko Temple that the artist's true name was Haruto Matazaemon, and that his death was recorded as having taken place in Edo on August 11, 1844. Then the discovery of the name Saito Jurobei on the program of a *nō* play given before 1825 seemed to spoil all the other "discoveries."

None of this searching has brought us closer to the artist of the magnificent prints that remain, nor has it given a direct clue as to why, after less than a year of print making, Sharaku vanished from the scene completely. The hundred and forty great prints that were produced between May 1794 and February 1795 are almost all large heads of popular actors from the three kabuki theaters: the Miyako-za, the Kawarazaki-za and the Kiri-za. Some smaller full-length actors, some scenes from the plays, a few *sumo* wrestlers, two historical scenes and some seventeen drawings, made perhaps for prints but never cut or published, are attributed to him. That is his entire output. Why a *no* actor would devote himself with such energy to a folk art considered vulgar by his own lord and company, we don't know. But for about ten months (some guess more by at least a half-dozen months) he was creating at the top of his power. There was no apprentice work, no fumbling into greatness. We find Sharaku at his peak with his first print and staying there.

We know almost all the actors he drew, the plays they performed and the dates and the theaters where they were playing. The actor's *mon*, or crest, is usually shown on his costume, and by comparing these portraits with pictures by other masters we know just what was going on in the Edo theaters that season when our young artist was active. (Or was he a middle-aged actor no longer able to perform the graceful steps of the classical courtly dramas—or even some sake-soaked old lecher dismissed in disgrace and now drawing these sketches to earn a few coins? There is no real evidence to date him properly as to age. The work is young; in his frenzy and his slashing lines he seems to be sardonic and bold with youth, full of irony and even boyish malice.)

Sharaku had no love of the actor's profession, at least not for the kabuki, and no respect for the mincing men who played the female parts or the pompous old windbags strutting before the admiring eyes of the customers, who would stop their chattering and the lifting of chopsticks from food bowls when their favorites came on stage. With a new skill Sharaku studied the faces, streaked white and crimson for character, the great headdresses of dead hair, the tasseled robes and sashes. He bared the innermost secrets of the eternal ego of the actor. For the first time in Japanese art we meet the naked human being; there is no formula here of pose and face, no accepted pattern of eyes and mouth, no mere ritual gesture worn thin and never changed. With Sharaku these charging, howling, declaiming actors become real people, and we can separate the parts they play from the men.

Do not expect in Japanese prints the lines of a Rowlandson or a Goya or a Daumier, the soft rounding forms of an Ingres or the brooding wash and line of Rembrandt. This is not Western art. There is no true anatomical detail, no feel of perspective, no cast shadows. With Sharaku the background is almost always just a blank, sometimes with a ground of mica or mother-of-pearl shell sprinkled over glue and soon cracking away. It is not with scientifically accurate anatomy, not with microscopic Dutch detail, that Sharaku gets his effect. The features of his actors follow no natural pattern, but flow wherever the artist feels they do the most good in projecting the mood or emotion he wants to register. The hands and fingers of his people baffle us at first, for they are not in proportion and are (by our thinking and training) badly drawn, with no bone or full muscle to give them shape. But in the portrayal of gesture, in forms and patterns, simplicity and subtlety of color, his drawings match our best; the final judging is in what these portraits of long-dead actors do to us, not how close they are to our own accepted systems of art. We must remember, as Sharaku knew, that systems are never absolutes, merely ground rules.

SHARAKU'S PUBLISHER

THE publisher of Sharaku's ukiyoye prints was named Tsutaya Juzaburo, and called Tsuta-ju for short. He was a round butterball of a man, always in a sweating hurry, always talking very fast, ready with a joke or a dirty remark, telling about something he believed in with a high, shrill voice close to panic, and with much laying on of hands. His lack of restraint, sense of risk, his active aggression were well known. His print shop was not one of the biggest ones, just a sort of square box stuck in next to the Miyako-za kabuki theater. With the doors removed one could walk into the shop itself almost as part of the street. Three walls were hung with colored woodcut prints; more prints were piled on tables, along with volumes of love poems and novels illustrated with delightful or gory scenes. An assistant would be trimming prints with a sharp tool, and in the back room would be more bundles of prints tied with ribbons, an engraver making some last-minute change on the block of cherry wood before him, and a printer, his arms dyed red and fingers blue to the knuckles, shaking his head over a proof sheet of damp mulberry pulp paper, pointing out where the cutter had failed to match the color blocks correctly. And always Tsuta-ju himself standing among his hired help, about to fight, shout or strike a blow, or run forward into the shop to bow to some samurai

SHARAKU

wanting a set of prints of *The Forty-seven Ronin* or an erotic series on the art of love, although samurai were forbidden to go to the common people's print shops, which from time to time felt the heavy hand of the censor.

Tsuta-ju was not a very successful print publisher compared to the men who handled more conventional and popular artists. But he had an eye and a flair; he had discovered the great Utamaro, and now he had a new young man whose prints caused the publisher's fat face to break into a closed-eye neigh of satisfaction, excitement and pleasure. Ah, where could you find anyone as great, as new, as different, as amazing, as Toshusai Sharaku?

But the housewives, the courtesans, the geishas, the actors, the *bakuchi-uchi* (professional gamblers) and the merchants who bought prints at the equivalent of ten to sixteen cents each were not impressed. Most of the customers would ignore the startling Sharaku prints—large heads of actors, the twisted bodies of action drama, scenes from great plays. They would buy more pallid work: the graceful sensuality of a Harunobu or an Utamaro, pictures of cheerful children or of parties on the river with fireworks going off overhead.

One can imagine Tsuta-ju standing in his shop, holding his round stomach with both hands, rocking on his white-socked heels. To a new customer the publisher lifts his arms as servants come in with trays of food and drink from the nearby teahouse. "Let us all go into the back room," he says. "We are cutting one of the best prints. It shows the director of the Miyako-za theater delivering a prologue."

They finish the tea, the *Naku miso* pickles and the *seimbe* cakes in the back room. From the street comes the twanging discord of people chattering in front of the theaters, vendors' cries and the incoherent dirge of actors reciting somewhere behind thin walls.

The fat publisher, trying to be pleasantly blasé, waves a sleeved arm to the back of the room, blocked off by bales of paper. "Now, if you will favor this too poor place, we will watch the cutting of the print."

A flaccid, innocuous-looking old man wearing large, badly scratched Chinese glasses of soft crystal is in one corner of the room, seated before a low table on which a cherry-wood plank lies. He is smoothing a rice-paper drawing onto the plank, rubbing thin the paper, which he has attached to the block. The cutter does not look up,

SHARAKU

but continues to smooth the drawing on its wafer-thin paper. It has been made with a slim brush and night-black ink.

The cutter then takes up one of his little knives and makes a swooping, bold stroke into the picture, cutting through the drawing into the block of wood. He makes another, then another, and suddenly chips begin to fly. With an amazing speed and an almost careless skill that seem at every slash to destroy drawing and wood, the engraver proceeds to cut away the white part, leaving only the black lines. He picks up a special little knife, a triangular gouge really, and begins with a magical control of his fingers and a sharp knife edge to cut the fine, almost invisible grooves that represent hair on a certain part of the head.

The publisher points to another boxed-in corner of the room. "Now, there we have a print actually being printed. A full-length figure of the actor Ichikawa Komazo the Second."

They move over past obstacles and look down at another low table, six inches high in front and sloping almost to the floor in back. The block on this table is being smeared with a thick black paste on a wide brush.

"The paper to be used is made of the finest mulberry-tree pulp," says the publisher. "It has been sized with rice paste and alum. It has just the right amount of moisture in it. Oh, it costs like ten demons driving one to ruin."

The printer has placed a sheet of the paper over the inked block.

"Notice, please," says the publisher, "how he placed it with the little raised mark on the edge of the block toward his stomach. That is called the *kento* mark. Each of the other blocks, which will add a different color to the print, will have a *kento* mark in the same place. In this way the register of all the blocks of the finished print will be perfect. Every color is done on a separately cut block."

The printer, a very thin man with a few snags of teeth left in a thin, tight mouth, looks up in disdain. He is rubbing the back of the paper with his broad thumbs. Then, taking up a small pad sheathed in some smooth material, he begins to rub the paper at great speed.

The publisher says, "That's called a *baren*. It's covered with bamboo-sprout skin and is made of twisted bamboo twine. It gives a good grain to the print. Watch the great pressure applied to the print; it looks almost careless."

The printer turns to smile at them. He flips the sheet of paper off the inked block and holds up a black print of a strutting actor.

126. SHARAKU, Actor as a Young Girl

All of these actor prints are actual portraits of famous stage personalities. This one is a masterwork of subdued colors, composition and the use of abstract shapes.

14⅝″ x 9¾″, from the author's collection.

127.   SHARAKU, Actor Playing a Fish Peddler

The backgrounds were usually printed with a composition of glue and crushed mother-of-pearl shell, which always crumbled off after a short time.

14⁹⁄₁₆″ x 10″, from the author's collection.

128. SHARAKU, The Actor-Manager

For directness of statement and delineation of character, this magnificent print has not been surpassed. Its details are eloquent, yet appear almost effortless.

15¼" x 10", from the author's collection.

129. HIROSHIGE, Snow Scene

His greatest skill lay in finding the bare bones of objects and making them beautiful. Here a touch of brown, a slash of blue added to black and gray bring alive a winter.

8¹¹⁄₁₆″ x 13¹¹⁄₁₆″, **from the author's collection.**

130.   HIROSHIGE, Fireworks at Night

Nothing is wasted; even the knots and grains of the wooden block are used, to form the sky, in this artist's new way of looking at things.

13¼″ x 8¹³⁄₁₆″, from the author's collection.

131.   HIROSHIGE, Bird over Landscape

In one of his best prints, the artist here ventures to look at the world from a hawk's view, combining the patterns of feathers and snow in a startling vision.

13¼″ x 8¹¹⁄₁₆″, from the author's collection.

132. HIROSHIGE, Mountain Landscape

Hiroshige's method of getting the desired effect could be very complex. Here forms and colors overlap each other; a plate like this called for the greatest skill and delicacy in printing. With his followers this became mere trickery; and the great age of Japanese print making was over.

$8^{15}/_{16}''$ x $13^{3}/_{4}''$, from the author's collection.

"How many copies do you print?" the customer asks.

"After the artist gives us the added colors," the publisher says, "we cut one block for each color, and that may take another week or so. Then we print two hundred first-class prints at the most. After that the moisture in the colors swells and distorts the wood, and the print is not clear. It often takes twenty-five days to print an edition of two hundred first-class prints. Of course, some poor publisher may then buy a used-up block and go on printing up to a thousand copies. But these are bad prints and the lines of the nose and hair break down, so sometimes they chop out the damaged parts and slip in a new section of block and recut it. Also the cheaper printers use whatever color pot they have at hand, not at all what the artist has indicated. Believe me, honored sir, buy only in my shop and you will get first-grade prints from the original blocks."

SHARAKU

Hiroshige

JAPANESE
1797-1858

IN AMERICA AND IN EUROPE at the beginning of the twentieth century, the prime favorite of collectors of colored woodblock prints was Hiroshige, who was accepted then as having been the greatest of the landscape artists in the whole field of Japanese prints. He is known by various first names; perhaps the best choice is that used by his teacher, Toyohiro, who called him Utagawa.

Hiroshige, who lived in loose and changing times when the art had decayed into wildly grimacing portraiture, overripe color and shoddy subject matter, was indeed among the last to work with dignity and power. His portrayal—in simple, flat patterns—of rainstorms, waterfalls, clouds, the moss of green dampness, the sea itself, the sacred mountains, was certainly the work of a major artist; the nature he depicted was a nature filled with harmony. But his work is limited to landscapes, and, fine as it is, it is viewed today—when we can get a better perspective of it in relation to the entire history of the art—as the endpiece rather than the climax of ukiyoye.

The T'ang and Sung periods in China brought the Oriental landscape to greatness, and Sesshu (1420-1506) best expressed the form in Japan; but he was not a print maker. The early print makers treated landscapes skillfully and beautifully, but retained old symbols of clouds and trees, images of water and mountains, that soon became banal from overuse. It was Hiroshige who brought a fresh eye to this art form.

He was born in 1797, the son of a fireman with a salary of sixty bushels of rice a year, living in the fire station on Edo's Yaesu River. When his father died, Hiroshige, at the age of twelve, succeeded him in the hereditary office of fireman. He began to draw early and studied with the Kano school of screen painting, and soon became influenced by the Western use of perspective through the study of Dutch etchings. He mastered print making and took the name Utagawa. In 1831 he issued an album of famous places, some of which the American painter Whistler used as themes for his *Nocturnes*.

The next year Hiroshige became famous with his major life's work,

The Fifty-three Stages of the Tokaido Road, or Eastern Sea Route.
Never before had such remarkable landscape pictures been done in
Japan. The very fury of wind, the slanting beat of rain, the feather
softness of snow were captured with unique skill. Every facet of life
on the great imperial road and in its stations, or inns, was recorded.
Shinto processions, night slowly falling, wrestlers going to *sumo*
matches, rain hanging in trees, merchants carrying their trade goods,
coolies buffeted by weather, everything that was natural to lake and
mountain travel was put down with fine color and striking new draftsmanship. Hiroshige inspected the forms of nature and the elements
with more depth and drama than any Japanese before him. When, at
the end of the nineteenth century, this set of prints was seen in Europe
and·America, he was hailed as one of the great artists of the world.
Oddly enough (or perhaps not), the Japanese themselves, while admiring the Hiroshige prints, never rated them as high artistically as
did the West. Oriental art seeks to accomplish more than capturing the
look of a place or a person with clarity and exactitude. The classical
calm was, to many, missing from this artist's landscape work.

HIROSHIGE

He repeated his scenes, doing at least twenty different sets of the
Tokaido Road series alone. He did about five thousand in all. His
figure prints are fine, rich, well done, but as a draftsman of men and
women he was not the match of Hokusai, Utamaro and others who
came before him. His birds, however, are marvelously real. He trained
two sons-in-law, who became Hiroshige II and Hiroshige III; they
and a fake Hiroshige who appeared some years later were inferior
artists.

His work declined with age and addiction to drink, but not his
popularity. Other artists printed two hundred copies of a print; Hiroshige often had to print ten thousand copies. But, for all his success,
he often had trouble finding the means to buy his cups of warm sake;
his fees for prints were low because he produced too many, he drank a
lot and had family trouble. In 1856 he retreated inside himself and
took the Buddhist tonsure. Two years later he was dead, perhaps in
the great cholera epidemic raging then, and was buried in a Zen Buddhist temple in Asakusa.

Hiroshige knew well the isolation of time, the weight of space,
the weaknesses of human tissue confronted with the forces of nature.
He took the absurd accidents of the casual landscape and made them
over into splendid rhymes and patterned reason.

Daumier

FRENCH
1808-79

IT WAS THE TIME when the modern world was being born, the world of Balzac's *La Comédie humaine,* those novels of lust for power, fame and possessions, of the rise of the middle class. The old world of glory, of Napoleon, was setting out to die in its wonderful uniforms, its fur busbies and shakos and its prancing horses. The weathered soldiers with wild mustaches who had been in Spain and who had retreated from burning Moscow with the Grands Chasseurs were now marching to Waterloo. Honoré Victorin Daumier was seven during those stormy Hundred Days in 1815, and his family had just come up to Paris from Marseilles. Stocky, blond and observant, the boy just off the lumbering diligence became a citizen of Paris.

Of his father we know that he was a glazier who wrote bad poetry, and that he had brought his wife and only child to Paris—to an *hôtel garni,* a rooming house, most likely—to take his place as a new voice of France. He received some encouragement in his writing from a few *nouveaux riches,* and two or three thin volumes were printed. But Napoleon was soon gone, and the restoration of the monarchy destroyed any interest in his poems, Daumier's father felt. He said, "Politics have obscured the muses," and he went back to fitting in window glass.

Squalor lighted by a three-sou candle took over. He set his only child to work as a messenger in the Paris law courts. Here the boy, always sketching, had his first look at those men of justice he was to set down in close to a hundred lithograph prints and in many drawings and paintings. He saw the great game of cupidity played in the courts, the pitiful mockery of justice. He observed the fox-faced lawyers and the judges in their black gowns, who were usually seated under a painting of the Crucifixion, indifferent to His suffering as to the mistreatment of the wretched people who came before them.

It was a time of change in a world weary of marching off to gallant wars that had drained away the best youth of the nation. Now people wanted to settle down, make money and enjoy the easy pleasures. The boy, hurrying with legal brief and tort through the medieval labyrinth of the Montagne Ste.-Geneviève to contact some lawyer at a cheap table d'hôte or waylaying a victim of a court case outside the Mont-de-Piété, the municipal pawnshop, soon saw the full drama of this new world. He observed all: the *haut monde,* the sippers of *apéritifs* in the cafés, the charwomen, the speculators, the frugal little government *fonctionnaires.* Balzac—the literary twin of Daumier—was to record it perfectly, this world of ragged litterateurs, strutting actors at soirees, dazed absinthe drinkers in the dens of the Rue St.-Jacques, toughs dancing in the open air at the Closerie des Lilas, and Monsieur and Madame drinking a Marc de Bourgogne to celebrate the new ribbon of the Legion of Honor on a fat shoulder.

In this flabby world of material success and social-ladder climbing, Daumier was to find his subject matter. Between the poor begging and the newly rich army supply contractors arriving at performances of Meyerbeer's *Robert le Diable,* he would discover the modern society— "a world seeking gold and pleasure," as Balzac defined it, adding, "Take these two words, *gold* and *pleasure,* for a lantern and explore the great stucco cage of Paris." Daumier took a pencil instead of the lantern. It was a fertile atmosphere for a boy always drawing on scraps of paper, beginning to see in the human face symbols of men exploiting other men.

From the law courts he went into a bookshop as a clerk, but he was not much of a reader and his attention drifted to the prints of a more heroic age, gesturing soldiers, officers on horseback leading lancers on gray Polish plains.

It was decided Daumier would study art. His father took him to a patron of his poetry, the Chevalier Alexandre Lenoir, whose theory of art was summed up thus: "Anything that serves to elevate the soul, to give sharpness and nobility to one's ideas, should enter the education of the painter." From casts he taught Daumier all the known human expressions, but the boy found this sterile and drifted to the Louvre, which was full of loot from the museums and palaces of Europe. Here he devoted his time to studying classical sculpture, the great bound captives of Michelangelo, the active still lifes and busy scenes of Dutch and Flemish masters.

Although Daumier was to become a great painter and sculptor, he was at this time too poor to buy an etching press or canvas and paint,

Mᵈˡˡᵉ Etienne-Joconde Cunégonde Bécassine de Constitutionnel, indignée, suffoquée ébouriffée et rococofiée à la représentation d'Antony où ce polisson de Dumas a eu l'immoralité de se moquer de la noble famille Bécassine de Constitutionnel.

Au bureau chez Aubert, pass Véro Dodat

Lith. Delaunois, rue du Bouloy 18.

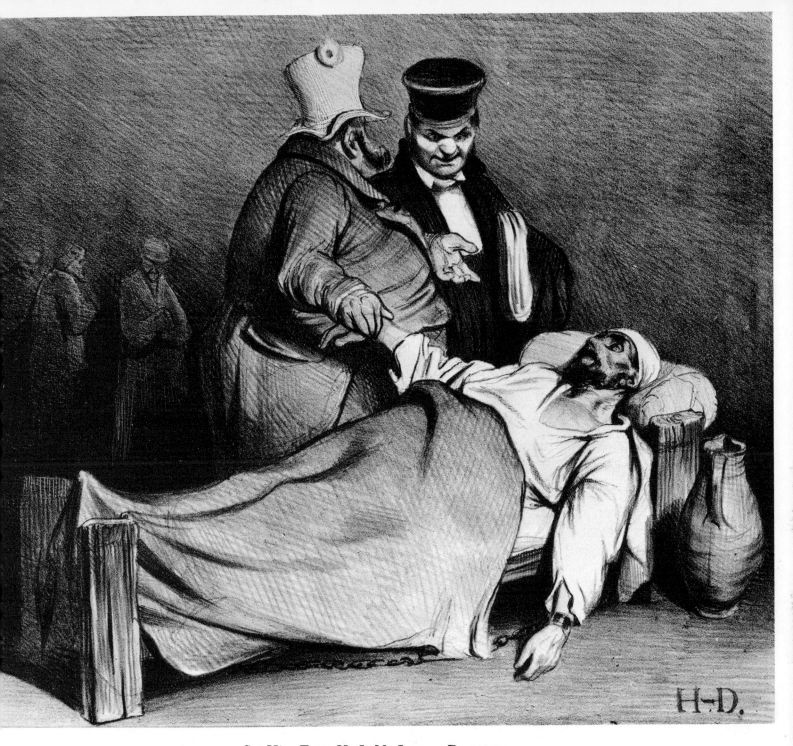

134. DAUMIER, Set Him Free, He Is No Longer Dangerous

The fat king tells his Minister of Justice this wry fact about the already dead political prisoner. For prints like this Daumier himself served six months in prison.

Lithograph, 8¹³⁄₁₆″ x 10¹⁄₁₆″, from the collection of George Longstreet.

133. DAUMIER, In the Box

As a young man, Daumier was scathing in his attacks on political reactionaries. This gross figure is his symbol for the venal journalism of the time.

Lithograph, 13½″ x 10⅜₁₆″, from the Helen Wurdemann collection.

Madame Etienne Goconde Cunégonde Bécassine de Constitutionnel, indignant, choking, scandalized and rococofied, at the performance of *Antony* in which that rogue of a Dumas had the indecency to ridicule the noble family of Bécassine de Constitutionnel.

135.   DAUMIER, The Accused Can Now Have His Say

This is the most brutal of the artist's attacks on the law courts and the lawyers of France. Ironically, today these prints are great favorites with lawyers, who collect them for their walls.

Lithograph, 8⅛" x 11¹¹⁄₁₆", from the collection of George Longstreet.

so he took up lithography, a new way of reproducing a drawing directly from the surface it was drawn on, a flat white stone. It would be pleasing to say he was a genius at draftsmanship from the start, but if we accept as his work certain prints signed "H.D.," which he may have done at fourteen or fifteen years of age, we are compelled to admit that as yet he showed little talent. The subject is still the banal one of soldiers; the composition and the drawing are poor. We do not find the great dexterity of line, the sardonic directness of his reading of human faces. That was all yet to come as he swallowed coffee and *croissants* and drew.

Just before the Revolution of 1830, Daumier began to work for the publishing firm of Aubert and Philipon. More established artists were already working for them, reproducing their work in woodcuts and lithographs—many colored by hand, for the color press was a long way off.

Charles Philipon is a character taken directly from the fashionable novels of the period. A go-getter, a pusher, a floater of companies to promote his publications, he would fit in today with the best of the hucksters or the publishers of weekly picture-and-news magazines. Of Philipon's many ventures, Daumier was to become connected with two, *La Caricature* and *Charivari*, the latter to be his meager meal ticket for almost forty years, during which it published literally thousands of his best lithograph prints. Daumier suddenly came to life, an artist still young, now vital and industrious in his attacks on the Bourbon regime.

His vision was clear, he saw how the parts make up the whole and how the whole (if an artist is in a proper relationship to his material) outlines the parts. Even his early work for Philipon shows Daumier as having an immediate sense of life, intuitive and tragic, under the comic masks of his characters. He knew he had some firm purpose besides that of earning a living, and he outlined with ridicule the wrongs of his time. Yet he managed to communicate sympathy and understanding, no matter how sharply he was lampooning the King, his judges and the vultures feeding on citizens. With an absurd simplicity (or so it appeared), he heightened human perception to the values of his time.

King Charles x favored a court grasping for everything portable and salable and encroached steadily on the rights of the citizens. In July 1830 he signed four ordinances, one of them curtailing the free-

DAUMIER

dom of the press. The July Revolution followed, and the King was replaced by a royal cousin who flew the Tricolor, kissed Lafayette on the cheek and set up a constitutional monarchy as Louis Philippe, the Citizen King. The regime was called *le juste milieu,* the happy mean. Very little was really changed, and Philipon in his *La Caricature* threw his artists into the battle against the new King. Philipon was an idea man, a milker of other people's brains, but he got results. Daumier said of him, "Without him to drive me, I wouldn't have accomplished anything." Not true, but one says things like that about a boss. He did get Daumier thrown, for six months, into the Ste.-Pélagie prison (once a convent, then a debtors' jail, and at the time a catch-all for politicals) for drawing the King as a pear-shaped symbol of greed labeled "Gargantua" and being fed the wealth and products of France by lines of little men.

After his release, Daumier did a print called "Souvenir de Ste.-Pélagie" in which the standing figure of a stocky young man is supposed to be Daumier himself. We see here a youth well prepared to take the blows of the world, his hands in his pockets, a grimace of ironic amusement on his face—the kind of person who does his job in the world as he sees it. He went back to attacking the King as an ungainly, greedy pear, his ministers and judges as devouring wolves; the faces and stances of these men, doomed to be forgotten, are remembered today mostly the way the young artist flung their images onto his drawing stones. He was now working for *Charivari,* a daily newspaper.

The street revolutions and the cries of *"Cochon!"* and *"Voyou!"* went on; the good citizens kept to their homes, the young hotheads died at the barricades, massacres took place. There was an attempt on the life of the King (several other people were killed, but not he), and a control was set up over the makers of engravings and lithographs. It was goodbye to free political scalping in art.

While Louis Philippe reigned, until 1848, Daumier turned to social satire, becoming the historian of society, its high and low scenes, the people at play and in misery. He cast a cold, calm eye on the battle of the sexes; he showed the seamy side of marriage (although he himself seems to have been happily married to the daughter of a glazier). He pictured the cafés, the studios of the artists, the gleaming greed of landlords, the pickpockets, the corruption of the law courts, the habits of maidservants and fat merchants.

DAUMIER

136. DAUMIER, P-s-s-t!

The original caption, "P-s-s-t!," had to be changed for the public distribution of this print. And the brothel mistress became a midwife.

Lithograph, 9⅞" x 7 9⁄16", from the collection of George Longstreet.

137.   DAUMIER, Music at Home

Daumier liked to depict middle-class life; he was the Balzac of print making. Here a family and their friends give a concert. The effect of lamplight is very skillfully suggested.
Lithograph, 8¼″ x 13¹³⁄₁₆″, from the collection of George Longstreet.

138. DAUMIER, Café Politics

The artist loved to make little clay heads and draw from them. This beautiful print shows his remarkable ability to portray faces full of strong character tinged with self-contentment.

Lithograph, 8¹³⁄₁₆″ x 10¾″, from the collection of George Longstreet.

139.   DAUMIER, The Happy Audience

One of the greatest of Daumier's prints, done in his mature years. Here he draws boldly on stone the convulsed features of the human face as he saw it.

Lithograph, 9%⁄₁₆″ x 8⅞″, from the collection of George Longstreet.

140.   DAUMIER, Discussion in the Gallery

Only Michelangelo before him was able to put so much swirling vitality into a group of animated figures. The solidity of form and the passion of expression are the work of a great master.

Lithograph, 9⅜″ x 8¹¹⁄₁₆″, from the collection of George Longstreet.

His first big popular success was a series of lively prints based on a character whom the actor Frédérick Lemaître had made famous on the stage, a gay con man called Robert-Macaire—jolly, ruddy-faced, glib, always ready to fleece an easy mark, always on the make for a sucker. The *Robert-Macaire* series was a huge success. Philipon claimed credit for the ideas, and he certainly wrote many of the long, dull captions full of puns. Philipon may well have been outlining a self-portrait: imaginative, greedy, not worried by idealism. He too was the symbol of the opportunism of his time.

Later, as Daumier mellowed, he not only reduced heroes to bourgeois but made the bourgeois heroic. The French poet Baudelaire wrote of him, "No one has known and loved as he has the bourgeois—that last vestige of the Middle Ages, that Gothic ruin with such an indestructible life, that type that is both so banal and so eccentric. Daumier has lived intimately with him, has spied on him day and night; he has learned the secrets of his alcove, he has become the intimate of his wife and his children."

DAUMIER

Daumier recorded history as an artist, not as a journalist. He felt that the past is important to someone—if only, as yet, to the artist; he saw the mind, consciousness, as a reservoir of time. There are no real riverbanks, Daumier sensed. You create them in time and store them in space. Art is a collection of rituals and habits to be hunted out, nailed down and transformed into intellectual essences called, in this case, prints. He was aware of the decay in his age, but to him decay was also a time to plant seeds for others.

On the surface Daumier led a simple, quiet existence, painted for his own pleasure, exhibited a bit, smoked a well-colored pipe, liked music and the theater. If the serious side of his art had no public fame, he had good friends in Courbet, whose studio he visited on the Rue Hautefeuille over the Café de la Rotonde, and Delacroix, who delighted in copying his drawings. He was a solid citizen working on his stones in a plain gray room with a stove and some rickety chairs; there were no valuable works of art or luxury. When Napoleon III (Victor Hugo called him "Napoleon the Little") set up the Second Empire, Daumier went on recording a society rushing to its final debauch in war; the Empress Eugénie had said, "My son will never be emperor if there is no war."

So war came, and France fell, and Daumier, old, his eyes failing, drew the most powerful history of the disasters of war since Callot and

141. DAUMIER, The Empire Is at Peace

In his old age the artist saw Napoleon III let France be torn to bits in its war with her eternal enemy, Germany. This is his statement of total defeat.

Lithograph, 9¹⁄₁₆″ x 7⁵⁄₁₆″, from the collection of George Longstreet.

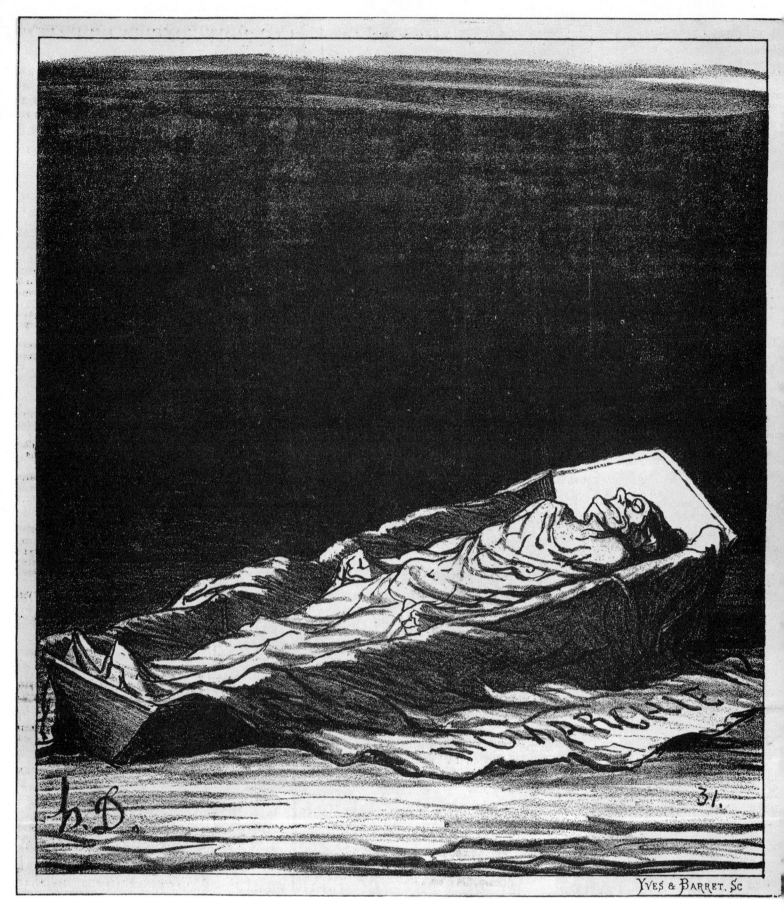

142.   DAUMIER, End of the Second Empire

This is almost the last print Daumier made. He was going blind; the dark memory of his country's defeat and the knowledge of his own failing eyesight are here expressed in somber, deep blacks.

Lithograph, 9 9/16" x 8 7/16", from the Helen Wurdemann collection.

Goya. His style became the simple black stroke, a scrawl of an angry stick of crayon, dropping all tricks of print making, all artistic trimming. On stone after stone he drew the pomp and hollowness of military minds, the dying moments of the war's victims, a desolate, burning landscape with a corpse or so on the ground. To this series of Franco-Prussian War prints he gave the simple text "The Empire is at peace."

It is in these last powerful prints that he merges his art with the greatness of forms found in Renaissance art. ("There is something of Michelangelo in this man," said Balzac.) He achieved monumental effects with human bodies in light and shade and became the greatest print maker of his time. Tragic, dramatic, almost drawn in gall, his prints portray both the dignity of man and his wretchedness created by his own hand.

There were times when Daumier was unemployed, "out of fashion," and he had nothing to eat. His eyes finally failed him, and he might have died like a blind dog under a Paris bridge. But the painter Corot let him use a little cottage, and there, aged seventy-one, Daumier died in 1879.

Baudelaire, whom we have quoted before, said of him, "Daumier's distinguishing note as an artist is his certainty—and, it should be added, a love of his suffering fellow creatures."

DAUMIER

Whistler

AMERICAN
1834 - 1903

JAMES ABBOTT MCNEILL WHISTLER spent so much of his butterfly-signed life being a public wit that he did not make the most of a great talent and a certain touch of genius in the making of etchings. He never fully realized what he might have become as an artist; yet his studied pose of indifference may have been merely the style of the last decades of the nineteenth century. It was a period that was symbolized by his slim shape, his gold-headed cane, the one white lock of hair carefully disarranged on his white forehead. One sees Whistler in the yellow-green gaslight of the period, reciting those bon mots shared with Oscar Wilde (which have been too often repeated). He endured his gifts as well as his failings; if he was dandified, malicious and insulting, he was also tough and heroic when fighting against great odds.

He was born in Lowell, Massachusetts, and attended West Point as a young man, but never graduated. In 1855 he was in England; then he studied in Paris with Gleyre. He settled in London to etch and paint. An artist of aggressive pride, he was much influenced by the etchings of Rembrandt and later by Japanese prints. He etched a magnificent early series of docks and riverscapes of the Thames around Chelsea and other districts of London, working subtle poignancy into his lithographs with a dreamy, evanescent effect.

It was while Whistler was living in Paris that Japanese woodcuts became the rage. Inside a shipment of porcelain from Japan was found a volume of prints which had been used as packing material. The prints found their way to an engraver, and from this incident came the myth that Japanese color woodcut prints were introduced into Europe as wastepaper. Whistler was in the lead, together with such artists as Degas, Monet, Fantin-Latour and Mary Cassatt, in making use of this new print art. There was a French Japanese society that met every week; it served Japanese food in Japanese ceramics, and everything but the cigars were Japanese. Whistler became an *arrangeur* of Oriental compositions. He felt it was an art that suited him, an

143.   WHISTLER, Thames Set: Limehouse

The stark freshness of this plate may be lost on us because so many inferior artists since Whistler's time have used the same style and reduced it to a banality.

Etching, 5″ x 7⅞″, courtesy of the Metropolitan Museum of Art, Dick Fund, 1917.

art of spacing, aided by color and dictated by mood. He used only twelve colors in his palette and drove everything into trailing wispy tones of silver and gray. In his prints there is more than a hint that he has taken the Japanese sampans, harbors and boating scenes and brought them over to become Westminster, Hungerford and Battersea. He gained in the ability to make the silhouette carry his forms.

Whistler as an artist was like certain lower organisms waiting in some pretty pool for pleasure, food and stimulus to drift their way, expecting in chance acquaintance a new world that presents no bills. Always the butterfly, changing from one shape to the other, he impressed the critic Meier-Graefe as being four persons: Englishman, Frenchman, Japanese, Spaniard. Certainly the English part did little for his art; Manet did a lot for his line; the Japanese prints taught him composition and color; and behind his dark, moody atmospheres created from night and soot emerge the features of Goya. Only rarely did all this merge into the work of a top-ranking artist. He spoke too well, and words are easy when art is hard. How much better to see his work without his jeweled prose: "Mist covers the riverside with poetry, as with a veil, and the poor buildings lose themselves in the dim sky, and the tall chimneys become campanili, and the warehouses are palaces in the night, and the whole city hangs in the heavens, and fairyland is before us . . ."

Yet he was an artist with an exquisite sensibility, an acute and inquisitive intelligence; but he persisted in stretching it to the finest point of fastidious refinement, until it tore. Whistler was aware that life is a wild tangle and yet art can be an orderly unity, that the artist can create a work that is crystal-clear but still seem convincing and basically related to the disordered reality. He worked to reconcile reality and imagination, but he knew that was not all; the true artist reconciles fact and form. This was the major problem of the artist at the end of the nineteenth century. Since then other ideas have been put forward, but even in his time Whistler was aware of the danger of too fast a journey away from the whole history of art. He suspected those jumping jacks of new schools of art who hurl themselves into the future, and who in the end fall to the floor like winter flies.

The art critic Ruskin called him "a coxcomb . . . flinging a pot of paint in the public's face." Whistler brought action for libel and won only an empty, token victory in the famous trial that followed; yet he did win, and then went gaily bankrupt. The defense, with a

WHISTLER

144. WHISTLER, Thames Set: Rotherhithe

The artist did a remarkable series of Thames River scenes, working for boldly realistic detail yet composing abstractly, as he had learned from the Japanese prints. The unexpected cutting off of figures and objects was new to European etching.
Etching, 10⅞″ x 7⅞″, courtesy of the Metropolitan Museum of Art, Dick Fund, 1917.

145.   WHISTLER, Thames Set: Hungerford

Unlike modern print makers, most of whom do not print their own work, Whistler was proud of his ability to use the etching press. The careful attention given to biting and wiping shows in the richness of this plate.

Etching, 5⅜″ x 8⅜″, courtesy of the Metropolitan Museum of Art, Dick Fund, 1917.

146.   WHISTLER, Thames Set: Longshoreman

It was in such early prints as this that Whistler continued the school of etching begun by Rembrandt. The quality of the line holds its own with the subject matter.

Etching, 5^{15}⁄$_{16}$″ x 8⅞″, courtesy of the Metropolitan Museum of Art, Dick Fund, 1917.

bourgeois contempt for art, had boldly stated, "The term 'coxcomb' used is not libelous but carries the old idea of licensed jester. . . . Mr. Whistler should not complain because his pictures are capital jests which have afforded much amusement to the public." He was awarded a shilling in damages, which he wore on his watch chain as a medal of victory. He was almost more notorious than famous, a man of talent marked for estrangement.

If his print making had a single striking feature, it was his obsession with doorways. Print after print is sometimes little more than a wall opening, a dark square into some remote house. From the beginning one finds in the prints cartouches of doorways, portals, gates, stone doorposts, fanlights; doorways off center or centered. Perhaps there was a doorway—some emotional block—he could not get through, some obsession of an exile in a far place. In 1903 he died and was able to go through the last doorway with a kind of scandalous fame as a poseur, a *flâneur*, which still clings to him. The prints

WHISTLER

147. **WHISTLER**, Thames Set: Eagle Wharf

Whistler understood the proper use of white or blank space in his prints. The thing we remember about this plate is not the well-etched details but the blankness which is a perfect representation of calm water.

Etching, 5⅜″ x 8⅜″, courtesy of the Metropolitan Museum of Art, Dick Fund, 1917.

148.   WHISTLER, Thames Set: Westminster Bridge

Composition for the artist extended beyond subject matter to the very shape of the copper he was working on. On a full-sized plate, this etching would not be impressive. It is the narrow form, repeating the bridge's shape, that makes the print outstanding.

Etching, 2⅞" x 7¹⁵⁄₁₆", courtesy of the Metropolitan Museum of Art, Dick Fund, 1917.

survive, with their clean surface tone and the dashing use of the drypoint burrs attacking the copper plate like swordsmen.

He was among the first of those Americans who felt they could not be happy or creative in their own crude land. Sargent, the portrait painter, Henry James, the Civil War draft dodger, the daffy Steins, Thomas Wolfe wallowing in Nazi Germany, T. S. Eliot of Missouri learning to carry a furled umbrella, all followed in the track of exile set up by James McNeill Whistler, the Moses of a flawed Exodus, who could say, along with Eliot:

> *Do I dare*
> *Disturb the universe?*
>
> *I know the voices dying with a dying fall*
> *Beneath the music from a farther room.*
> > *So how should I presume?*

149.   WHISTLER, Venice Set: Bridge

The sun of Italy and the impact of the impressionists carried Whistler away from the
realism of his early prints. Here, suggestion overcomes what might have been confusion.
Etching, 11¾″ x 7⅞″, courtesy of the Metropolitan Museum of Art, Dick Fund, 1917.

150.   WHISTLER, Venice Set: Nocturne

Borrowing a term from music, Whistler suggests a mood with muted forms and without use of detail. Held sideways, this print could be accepted as a fashionable modern abstraction.

Etching, 11⅝″ x 7⅞″, courtesy of the Metropolitan Museum of Art, Dick Fund, 1917.

151. WHISTLER, Venice Set: Doorway

The Freudians have been intrigued by Whistler's many etchings of doorways. How skillfully he has managed to capture our interest here with what is little more than an ordinary portal.

Etching, 11½" x 8", courtesy of the Metropolitan Museum of Art, Dick Fund, 1917.

Who are you indeed who would talk or sing to America?
Have you studied out the land, its idiom and men?
WALT WHITMAN

WINSLOW HOMER, considered by many to be our most original native artist, was born in Boston in the year 1836, into an America that still echoed to the sound of the frontier ax and the Kentucky rifle; the most beautiful postcolonial art form was the sleek hull of the clipper ship. The nation was still a country of farmers and forest runners, still beating westward past St. Joe on the Big Muddy and the Rockies and the land of the hairy mountain men. Some ladies in secret dipped snuff, a collation supper did not feature the cocktail, and the sachems of the Shawnees had not yet conceded they had lost the long war for the continent against the white weavers, smiths, tanners, coopers, distillers and hunters.

Homer's folks were old Yankee stock going back on these shores to the seventeenth century—middle-class people, careful of a dollar. The young man was attracted to art under the influence of his mother (her good, placid water colors still survive). At nineteen he was apprenticed to a local lithographer to help design labels and the simple advertising art of the period.

Art in the America of village whittlers and wooden clockworks was at the tail end of a depleted romantic period. Its good early artists had been Copley and Stuart and their school, who formed an appendage of the sleek British portrait mills. The panoramic Hudson River group with its dreamy, bosky landscapes was still active; art was at peace in a provincialism free of the new demands for naturalism across the sea in Paris. It was not fertile soil for original artists with sensitive ideals. Whistler and Sargent escaped abroad and sold their birthright for high tea and social comfort. Winslow Homer stayed and studied the genial, sentimental genre art at home, the simple patterns of corn huskings, and darkies strutting the cakewalk, the buffalo hunters, Thanksgiving on the farm and ladies in wide skirts that admitted of no legs.

At twenty-one Homer became an illustrator of the passing scene, mostly for the popular picture magazine *Harper's Weekly*. His drawings were done on wooden blocks coated with white, which were

Homer

AMERICAN
1836-1910

152.   HOMER, Sharpshooter

The artist served as an artist-correspondent in the American Civil War; this striking print is an example of his direct, realistic style.

Engraving, 9⅛″ x 13¾″, from the author's collection.

turned over to engravers who cut the drawings for printing. Soon he was settled in New York, depicting the gentry's carriages in Central Park, the pretty girls skating, the traffic of the streets. His full-page prints, as they appeared in the magazines, were the first native work to have originality and a power to match the country's sense of progress, its get-up-and-go. Rough-cut at first, the prints are the work of a vital self-taught artist still learning.

> *To the drum-taps prompt,*
> *The young men falling in and arming . . .*

In 1861 the war that was to turn a nation of farmers and craftsmen into a commercial world power sounded off with bronze guns attacking Fort Sumter. Homer went to the front for *Harper's Weekly*. He

153. HOMER, Thanksgiving in Camp

Homer avoided the heroic battle scenes so popular in his day, and he showed the soldier as he really lived most of the time, bored by camp life.

Engraving, 9⅛″ x 13¾″, from the author's collection.

drew almost none of the brave and false pictures of romantic battle charges. His nonheroic prints of camps and soldiers behind the lines, of the minor incidents and accidents of war, are, next to Brady's photographs, the most authentic record we have of the Civil War G.I. Joes. His prints of the wounded and the sharpshooters, of bull sessions around fires, of broken lances and lazy days in the dusty camp, all capture the true boredom and the sudden turn to legal murder that is war.

Returning from the front, Homer attended a few night classes at the National Academy of Design in New York and studied for a short time the art of oil painting with Frederick Rondel, a French artist who seemed unaware of the great impressionist excitement going on in Paris. Homer toiled hard on his prints and paintings, working in the

154. **HOMER**, A Parisian Ball

This and the next print are the result of the artist's short stay in Europe. He remained uninfluenced by contemporary styles abroad, but this composition is as action-filled as anything Toulouse-Lautrec was to do thirty years later.

Engraving, hand-colored, 9⁹⁄₁₆″ x 13¹¹⁄₁₆″, from the author's collection.

open air direct from nature. His success was small and he often announced he was through with art; his brother Charles would secretly buy his work to make Homer feel he had a following. The artist lived in New York for twenty years; he did many charming prints of its streets and people, but he never painted it. Sometimes he went wandering, alone and lonely, around New England, upstate New York, Virginia, North Carolina, hunting, fishing, weathering in the smoke of campfires, sketching the leaping trout, the shaggy gear of guides and their wall-eyed coon dogs.

The few photographs of him during this period show us a short, lean man with an aquiline nose over the long mustaches of the times. He looks reserved, taciturn and aware of the need for personal dignity. He was reported to be a dandy in city dress, and an early friend adds,

155. HOMER, Dancing at the Mabille, Paris
The artist gives no hint, in his title, that this is the notorious cancan.
Engraving, hand-colored, 9⅜₆″ x 13¹¹⁄₁₆″, from the author's collection.

"He had the usual number of love affairs." In a few years he was to
turn into a grim, antisocial hermit, the result, some claim, of one of
these love affairs: "He could not afford to marry the girl. He lacked
money to set up a household." But that was all to come yet; now he
was drawing the American girl, the first artist of talent to glorify the
long-stemmed American beauty, watching her playing croquet, pick-
nicking, bathing in the sea ("Perhaps not *quite* refined," someone said
of one of his prints of big-hipped dripping girls wringing out their
woolen suits). He pictured her in flounced skirt and puffed sleeves,
twirling a parasol, an innocent goddess with a roving eye. Tall, stately,
sure of herself and of her family's holdings in pork, real estate or textiles, she is ready to invade Europe, to dominate the American male
and drive him to greater efforts in business. Many of these pictures al-

156. **HOMER**, Winter

Here the artist gives free rein to the admiration he had in his youth for the beauty of young girls. Later he became a misanthrope because of an unhappy love affair.
Engraving, 9″ x 13⅝″, from the author's collection.

most duplicate the work Manet and others were doing in France. But Homer was as yet innocent of their sunlight on women's bodies; he had yet to see one of their paintings. It was his own early sensual drive, before bitterness set in, that created a vision of American girlhood which no other artist had produced.

There was another side to Homer. When disappointed in love, he turned to an America he was to record just before it passed with the buffalo and Johnny Appleseed and the beaver top hat. He was the poet of the uncouth farm, the country crossroads, the little red schoolhouse. He pictured life in the rough fields during harvest, haying, the realism of barefoot boys playing crack-the-whip, whooping at the seaside, shucking their clothes for the swimming hole. With Yankee candor and lyric naturalism, Homer illustrated the world of Mark Twain, of Thoreau and even Emerson, the world of the one-horse shay, Hudson

157. HOMER, On the Beach

Another example of the artist's fascination with young women. Later, the brooding sea became his one subject, and usually he eliminated the human figure.
Engraving, 9⅛" x 13¾", from the author's collection.

River Steamboat Gothic, the pink girls at Long Branch on the Jersey coast standing in their summer dresses with their backs to the warm wind.

He was not a man to talk much theory of art or philosophy of form. With a New England twang he once said, "If a man wants to be an artist he should never look at pictures." Yet his own sensual decorative panels suggest the secrets of the Japanese prints which he studied in the collection of his friend John La Farge. The flat pattern, the two-dimensional linear style, the simplicity of composition, all point to a close knowledge of Japanese decorative techniques.

When he was thirty, in 1866, Homer spent ten months in France. This stiff American, by now tight-lipped and wary, showed two paintings at the Universal Exposition in Paris. He did some work that showed little influence by the impressionist artists, but there was a

158. HOMER, Waiting

*This amazingly modern-looking composition is almost surrealist in its stark design. Its
figures suggest the lonely people we find later in de Chirico and Picasso.*
Engraving, 9¾₁₆″ x 13⅝″, from the author's collection.

lightening of his colors. Those who see the brushwork of Manet in his
work are unaware that he had been experimenting with the loose brush
long before going to France.

In 1873 he took up water-color painting and was elected to the National Academy. A few years later he was in England drawing the sea
and the powerful, classical bodies of the fishergirls. It was in many
ways his farewell to the love of women, and to the hurly-burly life of a
busy century rushing forward with new inventions and new discoveries, without a thought of what all this progress would cost.

At forty-seven Homer was a hermit, alone on the lonely Maine
coast at Prout's Neck, a storm-swept rocky peninsula jutting out into
the wild Atlantic. Here among boulders, sea spume, kelp and struggling pines he built himself a shack studio. He did his own cooking

159. HOMER, Gloucester Harbor

Most of Homer's woodcuts were engraved by crude local cutters, but in this series on boys at play he was fortunate in working with a master cutter. Here is one of the best of his scenes of childhood.

Engraving, 9⁵⁄₁₆″ x 13⁵⁄₁₆″, from the author's collection.

and housework. Sometimes he was driven out by winter, and beginning in 1890 he spent some winters in Nassau and in Florida, but he was reluctant to leave Maine, for his withdrawal to solitude and the sea satisfied him. He said, "The sun does not rise or set without my notice and thanks." He was a more rugged Thoreau, living on his sea-chafed shore and scowling away contemporary society.

An aging, bitter man, he did his last water colors with a startling brilliancy that revived the art and took it back from maiden aunts mocking a rose in a vase. He would still stop painting from time to time, but he always went back to it. In the end he removed the human form almost entirely from his pictures, concentrating on sea and rocks and the endless spinning water, distilling events of nature down to a few forms, a few colors. By the Maine sea he stayed and worked, to the

160.   HOMER, On the Bluff at Long Branch

This print led to the large paintings he did of windswept beauty. They suggest Manet and Monet, but in sharper focus.

Engraving, 8⅞″ x 13⅝″, from the author's collection.

sound of sea gulls gawking in the wind, till he died in 1910, at the age of seventy-four, as impassive as the boulder at Prout's Neck.

He had been a print designer for seventeen years, and his work in that field is mainly uncollected, still found in the old magazines where he, like Daumier, left some of his best work as a daily task done for survival and because he had to record his comments on history and society. If the early prints are crudely cut by ill-trained craftsmen, the later Civil War prints are among the most powerful ever done, things of startling beauty, controlled style and classical composition. He did his drawing for the prints from his sketchbooks and paintings, combining ideas and themes, so that most of the prints show an original side of an American artist who still needs further study to grasp his full importance. Actually it is in his prints and water colors, and not in his oils, that he stands out as a directly inspired native artist, the

161. HOMER, Gloucester Harbor

Another of the series of boys at play. The way in which the boat on the left has been cut off so boldly was probably the result of the artist's study of Japanese prints.
Engraving, 9⁹⁄₁₆″ x 13⅝″, from the author's collection.

home-grown genius reworking his own material in his own way.

That he withdrew from our society is perhaps a reminder that the honest artist was still not able to become fully part of the world around him. Most likely the stern New England core of the artist did not want to be swept up by the vulgarity of the Gilded Age or the expanding world of the robber barons. He might have been a happier man if he had gone abroad like Whistler to Montmartre, Henry James to Mayfair, Sargent to Paris, T. S. Eliot to Kew Mews. But Winslow Homer chose to stay in his homeland and draw his inspiration from it. If in the end he loved little of what his country had become, he did love the country itself, the fields of the republic, the trees, sand dunes and seas that patterned it.

> *Rise, O days, from your fathomless deeps,*
> *Till you loftier, fiercer sweep.*

Gauguin

FRENCH
1848-1903

No OTHER ARTIST has so been the victim of legend makers and fiction writers as Paul Gauguin. Beneath the man of myth is a serious and thoughtful Gauguin, whose numerous writings express his belief that the artist has three duties: first, to impose order on disorder and set up rational boundaries beyond which he dares not go, which is the function of the mind; second, to be true to his heart, which admits no boundaries and which yearns to pierce phenomena; third, to free himself of mind and heart in order to achieve the impossible. Beyond that, he was an artist of profound originality whose paintings, great as they are, may in time be overshadowed by the influence of his astounding approach to the modern woodcut print.

He was born in Paris in 1848, the year of the big wind and political shouting all over Europe. That year of turmoil forced his family to leave for Lima, Peru. The father died on the trip out, but the survivors of the brood lived in Peru for four years. The Gauguins claimed descent from the Borgia family of Aragon in Spain, and it was true that a granduncle had been Viceroy of Peru, one Don Pío Tustan y Morcoso. Judging by the artist's Indian features, there may have been native American blood in the family as well.

In 1865 young Paul became a cadet in the merchant marine (as did Manet), and he followed the sea till he went as a clerk, into the Paris offices of the stockbrokerage firm of Bertin's, in 1871. Two years later he became a speculator, a painter and a married man. His wife was a Danish girl named Metta Gad.

It is here that legend and fiction often take over. He was not a mere Sunday painter, but a greatly talented man who divided his time between the office and his art. He collected rejected geniuses: Manet, Cézanne, Pissarro, Renoir and Monet. He exhibited his own work at the Salon and was one of the artists showing at the Fifth Impressionist Exhibit in 1880, and later at the Sixth and Seventh. It was not until 1883, at the age of thirty-five, that he left off going to the office and devoted himself to full-time painting.

His wife, a chill blonde, didn't like it, but he did not cruelly walk out on her as legend claims. They had a large family and life was hard. Gauguin was dissatisfied with his time and with Europe. Its art was

162. GAUGUIN, *Offerings*

Today we accept this print as an artist's presentation of a mood in terms of a landscape with figures. In Europe it shocked and delighted a whole generation of artists with its dark masses and its directness. Munch based the style of many of his prints on Gauguin's new values.

Woodcut, 8 1/16″ x 14″, courtesy of the Museum of Modern Art, Lillie P. Bliss Collection.

changing, but although he had begun as an impressionist, nature in sunlight and air was not enough. He was closer to Huysmans' hero in *À rebours*, who said, "The age of nature is past; it has finally exhausted the patience of all sensitive minds by the loathsome monotony of its landscapes and skies." To repattern nature was Gauguin's first job, and he set to work hunting for a method.

Gauguin worked hard in cold studios, with a sick son, separated at times from wife and family, so hungry he took work as a billposter, so stubborn he would not paint in the popular style of the moment for any dealer. He rejected the theory of the social-minded that the arts are in trouble when beauty exists only for the artist. He soon saw that only the artist could invent new and original art, not the critic, not the dealer, and never the public. He felt that the artist had a duty to himself to seek self-realization – the projecting of his nature against popular taste. He disliked Europe; the norms of its society were no longer valid for him, and Kierkegaard's moral austerity bothered him as

163. GAUGUIN, The Gods (Te Atua)

In this print the artist blends the crude stone and wood carvings of native cults with his own reaction to them. The sensuality of the middle figure jars with the stark, symbolic quality of the others; perhaps it was intended, perhaps it was his Parisian past creeping in. But the unity of the composition holds.

Woodcut in black and ochre, 8″ x 13⅞″, courtesy Museum of Modern Art, Lillie P. Bliss Collection.

much as the mad rush for money. With Freud he could share "a sense of unease with civilization."

He had a few followers now who went with him in season to Brittany, where he would paint a picture on a door for a meal and talk of what interested him. The flat, solid patterns of his first style began to appear: yellow Christs, peasant women calmly watching a wrestling match out of the Bible. He developed a rugged, strong way with color that no longer aped the impressionists and their vague shapes in sun or gaslight. In 1888 he went to Arles to stay with his friend Vincent van Gogh, until the Dutch artist had an attack of madness and Gauguin left him.

His wife and children, while they found life hard as a painter's brood, lived in the hope of his giving up art. There never was one sudden and final domestic break; it was Metta Gauguin who left the now feverishly painting artist again and again and who made the final separation. She was tainted with a northern Protestantism, full of her own sterile virtue, that saw the Devil at work in all art forms. She cried

164. GAUGUIN, Night Eternal (Te Po)

The artist failed in his dream of becoming a true primitive in ideas and forms. He achieved something else: a private universe that is closer to William Blake than to the South Seas. Although the subject and composition are like Blake's, the style and cutting are his own. Woodcut, 8 1/16" x 14 1/8", courtesy of the Museum of Modern Art, Lillie P. Bliss Collection.

out, of her husband, "Art has made him a lying, perverted animal!"

Gauguin was one of those deluded people who feel that going away to a green, far-off island will solve all problems and give one a free, new life. A trip to Martinique in 1887-88 had aroused his love of the tropics, despite the fact that he had returned to France with dysentery and fever. The hunt for the dream island drove him, and in 1891 he sailed for Tahiti. He found there only some of what he wanted, and a great deal of what he didn't. The simple savage, the willing, free-breasted, slavelike woman, lived under colonial masters who demanded taxes, rigid order and a good twelve per cent for their stockholders. Two years later Gauguin was back in France, showing his island paintings at Durand-Ruel (which again shatters a legend that he was unknown during his lifetime). The Brittany group he had fathered, now called the Nabis, from the Hebrew word for *prophet*, were the avant-garde talk of the town. But his pictures did not sell, even if Gauguin was somebody. Meanwhile, Edvard Munch in Norway was making bold woodcuts based on Gauguin's ideas.

In despair, he went back to the South Seas to cut more of his woodcuts, paint pictures and reach the screaming end of his nerve cords. In 1898 he bungled an attempt at suicide. Two years later he launched a Tahitian newspaper with the aid of a stenciling machine. Its name was *Le Sourire, journal méchant,* and some of his finest woodcuts appeared in it. He was cutting into the flat surface of the board in the Japanese manner, making symbols of local gods and cults. Handcolored, these prints were like nothing ever done in the West, evoking the mystery of man and God while shaping primitive forms that were soon to shock and delight Paris as Negro and South Seas art were discovered, foreshadowing cubism. Gauguin—alone with a native wife, forgotten, deathly ill, his legs running sores, his heart acting up—went on perfecting his work and writing his strange texts.

GAUGUIN

His early writing, *Noa Noa,* an autobiographical novel, had been called "a romantic confection." But now he was deeper into Oceanian life and art. The local ideas of form could, he saw, provide a blend of perception and representation in his work, a blend that would create a new vision of two-dimensional space in his prints and canvases. Space free of stylish Paris studio talk, of that too glib intellectual conscience. He could now control his innermost self while waiting to mark down awe-inspiring presences.

Gauguin was still the hunter, still escaping, like Herman Melville, Robert Louis Stevenson, D. H. Lawrence. All had come or were to come this way, taken in a moment by the enchantment. All found it did not last, but they were able to get the taste of it into prose or paint. So Gauguin stayed, living not in native orgy or in laziness catered to by naked girls with pointed breasts, but with the real world rejected and rebuilt into art. His form became classical, close at times to Piero della Francesca with its archaic figures.

If only he could live at peace a few years more. But the Church, the judge, the police, all harassed the dying artist; the syphilis contracted long ago in Montparnasse made its inroads on the time he spent recording his final word to the world. On crude burlap he painted a long, long painting with a long title, a vast spiritual testament, "Whence Come We? What Are We? Whither Go We?" It was one of the times when Western artists have reached the summit on the subjects of love, birth and death.

His last actual picture was "Breton Village in Snow." The tropical sunshine on his trembling hands seemed suddenly not enough. He

165. GAUGUIN, The Locusts and the Ants

Try as Gauguin did, he could not shake off all of his past in the South Seas. The influence of the Japanese prints is clearly shown here. There are no shadows and the background does not recede in space.

Zincograph, 8⁹⁄₁₆″ x 10¼″, courtesy of the Museum of Modern Art, Lillie P. Bliss Collection.

wore out and died in 1903, and his old Maori friend Tivka said, "Now he is man no longer." He was gone, the man with an atavistic yearning for the primitive, the maker of woodcuts of Hina, the Tahitian goddess of the moon, this man with an abstract unity of vision who said, "Art is a foray fierce as men in battle."

He fathered much more than a few native sons in the straw huts. Fauvism and cubism took his ideas as their own. The Nordic woodcut artists, frozen out of the school of Paris, eagerly surrendered to his form. One finds him in German expressionism, in Edvard Munch's best work, among the *Jugendstil* artists, the Brücke group, the New

243

166. GAUGUIN, Title Page for "The Smile"

This print is almost a history of the artist: the lettering from the smart reviews of the 1890s, the emotional faces that hint at studio models, and the truly native animals styled like local carvings.

Woodcut, 4″ x 7³⁄₁₆″, courtesy of the Museum of Modern Art, Lillie P. Bliss Collection.

Munich artists. Kandinski's woodcuts echo Gauguin and lead at last to pure abstraction. The flat, flowing form, the mystic shapes that come from the inner eye, all that Gauguin invented, is now fashionable among New York's abstract nonobjective artists. What has not been taken over from him, not yet, is his vital interest in the myths of man himself. For by the middle of the twentieth century man had been flattened out into mere still life.

Gauguin had said, "There are noble lines, and there are deceptive lines." He himself, hunting a dream island, was unaware that someone had invented the concept of happiness out of pure reason and forgotten that mortality makes us sad. But Gauguin was aware of the reality which is not at all like nature. He worked in a serenity of spirit when doing his best work. He was not lost but he was always looking, he was not damned but he was aware of the deep dark below us. Like the poet Samuel Daniel, he questioned everything and tried to make art of it:

> *Are they shadows that we see?*
> *And can shadows pleasure give?*
> *Pleasures only shadows be,*
> *Cast by bodies we conceive.*

167. GAUGUIN, Wonderful Earth (Nave Nave Fenua)

There is nothing of Paris and the popular styles of the period in this woodcut. It is primitive in style but conceals great feeling. The artist shows his understanding of what a print should be, and he makes no attempt to use color in any form but simple stencils.

Woodcut printed in color with stencils, 13¹⁵⁄₁₆″ x 8″, courtesy of the Museum of Modern Art, gift of Mrs. John D. Rockefeller, Jr.

245

168.   GAUGUIN, Woman at the River (Auti te Pape)

Why hide the marks of the chisel, the grain of the flat board? The print becomes a blend of its material and the artist's reaction to it, together with the subject matter.

Woodcut printed in color with stencils, 8¹¹⁄₁₆″ x 14″, courtesy of the Museum of Modern Art, gift of Mrs. John D. Rockefeller, Jr.

"WHAT DOES IT ALL MATTER, as long as the wounds fit the arrows?" So Franz Kafka, the most searching of modern writers, summed up the reaction of the supersensitive man to his times. The artist Edvard Munch (pronounced Moonk) asked the same question in his own way. Munch, one of the most powerful artists of our time, is little known in this country; not much has been written about him in English. He was born in Engelhaug, Norway, near Leyten, in 1863. His greatest fame was achieved in Mittel-europa, at a time when the fashionable avant-garde felt that anything done outside Paris was not worth looking at. Munch's family were churchmen and historians. He was proud of his Norwegian past, and the only painting he did in Italy was of an uncle's grave in the Protestant Cemetery in Rome.

His father was a military doctor, who in 1863 moved with wife and children to Christiania, as Oslo was then called. He was an odd father, and the boy Edvard–frail, oversensitive–reacted to the nuances of nature and forms with a neurotic intensity and a born artist's temperament. The family disease was tuberculosis and the mother died of it when Edvard was five. The father, a religious fanatic, close to insanity, made the boy's life a combination of the Bible's Hell and Army physical punishment. The boy's favorite sister died of the white plague when he was fourteen, and the frail boy, sensitive and introspective, became obsessed with the themes of birth, love and death.

He was not of the stern stuff of ministers, historians *or* Army doctors, so at seventeen Munch was studying in the State School of Art and Handicraft. The most powerful of his early influences was Christian Krohg, a tough, realistic painter of harbor scenes whose style was much like that of Winslow Homer. From Krohg the young artist learned how to use a brush with dexterity. He taught himself how to make color and form take on some of his own emotional reactions to life. He agreed with Baudelaire, "Life being what it is, one must think of revenge."

The end of the nineteenth century was a great time of ferment, in

Munch

NORWEGIAN
1863 - 1944

169. GAUGUIN, Fragrance (Noa Noa)

One has to go back to the woodcuts of the late Middle Ages for anything this direct and simple. The style is not the refined one of "works of art," but that of the crude woodcuts printed on cheap newspaper. The artist has tried to purge himself of avant-garde *sophistication.*

Woodcut printed in color with stencils, 16⅝" x 10½", courtesy of the Museum of Modern Art, Lillie P. Bliss Collection.

which many problems could, the intellectuals said, be solved by scientific observation, by a new realism that admitted no romantic nonsense from the past. Darwin had the answers, Freud was beginning to probe the secrets of the unconscious, and Karl Marx, for many, was writing in the reading room of the British Museum the one true gospel for all times on the proper marching orders for the universe.

Munch was interested in the café and studio discussions where, in the thick of tobacco smoke, the talk was of Ibsen, Björnson and the yellow-backed novels of Zola fresh off the press. Ethical and social questions fired the artists; the creative mind required new freedom; art was a weapon; new sexual and moral values would make the world happier and healthier. Munch tried to swallow all this strong brew, but, sensitive to other values and deeper personal emotions, he reacted differently from his fellow artists. He went hunting for material in his own life and his own family. At first his major theme was women, whom he depicted in paintings, etchings and woodcuts; woman was to be a flower and a snakebite to him all his life, for Munch wanted love, devotion, perfect harmony, and partnership with an ideal creature. A shocker was the great painting and lithograph of a young girl, called "Puberty": the naked, slim, adolescent body and the fearing, unfocused eyes, the child-woman filled with awareness and anticipation. When Munch's fellow artists wondered at this startling subject matter he said simply, "Everybody can't be painting nails and twigs."

French impressionism was seeping up from Paris, and by 1889 Munch was in Paris, lightening his color, simplifying his forms. He also visited the Riviera and Italy, and he came back to Norway with the visions of van Gogh and Gauguin in his mind. He annexed Gauguin's flat shapes, his simple, direct drawing. Munch's final patterns were to become the main inspiration of much of the *art-nouveau* and *Jugendstil* schools in Mittel-europa. He painted and cut such prints as "The Kiss by the Window," "Anxiety," "The Shriek," bold new themes that were frightening in their power to invoke emotion from the viewer. "The Shriek" is mostly just a shouting head, mouth up, rings of sound surrounding it; it startled people to an awareness of what could be done with modern forms.

In 1892 Munch had a big Berlin show that led to controversy and fame. There were demands by powerful Academy groups that the show be closed as indecent, and it was. Munch had begun work on his cycle of paintings *The Frieze of Life,* and on many haunting etch-

170.   MUNCH, The Death Chamber

Everything Munch drew was autobiography. Some artists observe; Munch reflects himself in a mirror of his own design. This scene of fatal illness he witnessed several times. Is he the boy to the left, turning away but already full of the image?

Lithograph, 15¼″ x 21⅝″, courtesy of the Museum of Modern Art, gift of Mrs. John D. Rockefeller, Jr.

A mon ami Paul
E. Munch

171. MUNCH, The Young Model

When he painted this same subject he called it "Puberty." The artist was obsessed by women and made unhappy by them. To him the girl is an enigma, already in her first moment of womanhood. The simple, decorative nude is not for Munch.

Lithograph, 16⅛″ x 10¾″, courtesy of the Museum of Modern Art, Purchase Fund.

ings, lithographs and woodcuts. He painted his inner self, what was then called the soul—a soul that was stripped bare and full of wonder as it waited for its wounds. The German artists and critics admired Munch, who was neglected in Paris and unknown in America. He remained in Germany until 1908, becoming a great influence on the artists who were to produce German expressionism. Munch re-created in his prints love, death and the powerlessness of man to change his life patterns. He drew himself and the individual caught up in the time prison and the love act. Ecstasy, pain, the acts of passion, jealousy, fear and the anxiety of lovers were his themes. Nothing being done in Paris, where the story was to be the Fauves and cubism and its bolder offshoots, touched the personal, emotional level of Munch's best work. He drew woman as first innocent, then unobtainable, self-absorbed, and finally as either the great mother or the vampire. His famous set of prints *Women in Three States* appeared, all touched with pain and frustration, keyed above the usual German romanticism. He also added to landscapes the luminous, diffused northern skies, a mood that, together with his simple artistic means and two-dimensional decoration, was to compose the vocabulary of the new Central European schools of art.

MUNCH ·

Into his figures Munch put invitation and irony, overt symbols of his own inner tensions. Yet he was actually a charmer, a tall, handsome man, strikingly impressive with his large aristocratic features and poise. The self-portraits in his prints show the other side of him: a bitter, defiant man, an ascetic, somber lover of life, wary and on guard. He had the feral eye of suspicious men.

"Art is a crystallization," he said; a pure visual experience, his work hinted, refined to a final truth by subtle analysis, the inherent qualities of personal adventure exposed. He attacked print making like an explorer attacking a new continent. "Tingle-Tangle," his four-color lithograph of music-hall life, goes beyond Lautrec. Woodcutting was a technique he seemed powerfully drawn to, and one in which he was influenced by Gauguin's methods. He emphasized the wooden surface itself as part of the print. The signatures of the knife and the gouge were left in, producing strong, vibrant and varied areas that never failed him. Munch experimented with backgrounds of lightly inked grained wood, leaving in tree rings and knotholes. In color or in black and white, he was constantly extending his visions.

A desperate love affair almost destroyed Munch. Feeling that the

172. MUNCH, Anxiety

The world was too much with him; the artist could hardly face it, and yet he drew it, made many prints of its pain and terror. He is the first artist to suggest seriously that he had heard of Freud. Anxiety is not a modern disease but we seem to feel it more today, these neurotics tell us.

Lithograph, 16⅜" x 15⅜", courtesy of the Museum of Modern Art, Purchase Fund.

173. MUNCH, The Shriek

This is the most famous of the artist's prints. Not only does it suggest sound, but many viewers claim they can actually hear it. As art, this lithograph is startlingly new in its use of line to express a mood not drawn before. There is no change of texture to suggest that the sky is any kinder than rock or bridge.

Lithograph, 20¹¹⁄₁₆″ x 15¹³⁄₁₆″, courtesy of the Museum of Modern Art, Matthew T. Mellon Foundation Fund.

174. MUNCH, The Kiss

Munch drew, painted, etched, made woodcuts of this subject. This print has no romantic setting, no soft light to hide the reality of the moment. We do not belong here; a door has opened and given us a quick, stolen glimpse.

Aquatint and drypoint, 12⅞" x 10⅜", courtesy National Gallery of Art, Rosenwald Collection.

175. MUNCH, Two Beings

Munch was not ashamed of literary content in his work. But as pure art, this print—with its balancing of black and white, of forms rounded and forms simplified—would grip us regardless of subject matter.

Drypoint printed in black, 6⅝″ x 8⅞″, courtesy Museum of Modern Art, Phyllis B. Lambert Fund.

woman would ruin him as an artist, he tried to break away. What followed is so bizarre that only Poe could do it justice. The woman gave out the news that she was dead and had herself laid out for the grave, then rose and mocked her lover when he came for the burial. Later she fired a pistol at Munch and wounded him in the hand. Burdened by her neurotic harassment for years, the artist paid her not to torment him. He began to drink, sank deeper and deeper into alcohol, and was arrested in 1904 for fighting in a café. He exiled himself to Weimar in Germany, and after one four-day drinking spree he ended up in the clinic of the psychiatrist Dr. Daniel Jacobson. He was under treatment there for eight months. Free again, he did little drinking the rest of his long life.

MUNCH

Munch is a kind of transmission belt between the gay, décolleté subjects of the impressionists and the brooding sense of doom that artists were to feel in the twentieth century just before 1914. He helped destroy the clichés of a more hopeful time and bring a spontaneity of expression to the darker secret side of man. One looks at Munch's prints and feels a somnambulistic mood in which art is abandoned to memory, even to a kind of simulated paranoia hunting the second reality of a personal story. His work remains fine art, for Munch agreed with Chekhov, "It is sufficient for the artist to ask the right questions." And this Munch does.

In the end we accept Munch's work as normal to strange times. The anarchist, nihilist shocks in it have softened as our vision has become trained to accept his statements that look direct but have come through the processing of Munch's ideas and emotions. He wielded the print needle, the cutting tool, like a scalpel. He and his school won a great victory over the slick masters of his youth. Dead was the art of Meissonier, Winterhalter, Boulanger and the Salon favorites.

Munch was now aware that art is often a compensation for lost illusions. He continued to make his prints, he painted, he collected everything he had ever done and made copies of what he had sold. He lived surrounded by himself, worked constantly at the transformation of his patterns, at revaluation, reinterpretation; he had his symbols, and from now on he worked at refining and expanding them.

There were honors coming to the artist. In 1908 Munch was made a Knight of the Order of St. Olaf. Collectors presented large groups of his best work to the Norwegian National Gallery a year later.

Munch went back to drawing women, large, placid nudes, more

176. MUNCH, Tête-à-Tête

The artist's mood was not always grim. Here, the twinness of everything (except the pipe) accentuates the comic mood. The enigma of womanhood which obsessed Munch lurks behind the smoke—but he has left it at that.

Etching and drypoint, 8⅝″ x 12⅞″, courtesy of the Museum of Modern Art.

studies of the love motif but touched now with self irony. He began to use workingmen as models, the hills, harbors, bridges of his native land. The great trees, the powerful brown peasant bodies of men in the sun and at work, all were part of his creative parade. He settled down in Ekely, near Oslo, to stay there thirty years, a recluse who worked hard, traveled back over the past to France and Germany and Italy, but always returned to his studio. At seventy he said of himself, "The last part of my life has been an effort to stand up." He painted and drew with a drive toward life and vitality. It was now that Munch felt the truth of Kafka's lines: "You do not need to leave your room. Remain sitting at your table and listen. Do not even listen, simply wait. Do not even wait, be quite still and solitary. The world will freely offer itself to you to be unmasked, it has no choice, it will roll in ecstasy at your feet . . ."

His portraits of women took on a new inner strength, a sense of devotion. His work showed the integration of body and spirit of an artist who had made his peace with the world. "I am quite faded and classical," he said.

MUNCH

One of his last pictures shows a very old man, given to insomnia, wandering in an empty house between a giant floor clock and an unslept-in bed. He must have been amused when some of his best work was included among the great modern masters in the notorious Nazi exhibition of "degenerate art." He was eighty-one when he died in 1944, and the expressionism which he had helped father was emerging to challenge the long-entrenched position of the school of Paris.

177. MUNCH, Omega's Eyes

With gripping tension, the artist pictures the enemy: woman. The surface communication hits us at once, and the strange complexities of the artist's fears are clear. His style is blunt and unrefined; the image is inexorably fixed.

Lithograph, 16⅛″ x 12½″, courtesy of the Museum of Modern Art, gift of Samuel A. Berger.

178. MUNCH, Jealousy

This kind of statement is unfashionable in print making today. It is too personal a confession and perhaps overromantic in the art nouveau style. But it is also a very fine example of lithographic art, and intensely memorable to those who are not put off by its directness.
Lithograph, 18¾″ x 22⅝″, courtesy of the Museum of Modern Art, Purchase Fund.

179. MUNCH, Violin Concert

Even with as simple a subject as a concert, the artist conveys a brooding presence in these two women. Munch always seems to suggest a sleepwalker's irrationality, no matter what he draws. We know at once that he is Strindberg's fellow countryman.

Lithograph, 18⅞″ x 22″, courtesy of the National Gallery of Art, Rosenwald Collection.

Toulouse-Lautrec

FRENCH
1864-1901

THE LIVES of so many postimpressionists—Gauguin, van Gogh and Toulouse-Lautrec—have been so vulgarized and distorted by bad novels and trashy motion pictures that the real men are pulled out of shape and the true image of their work suffers from overadvertisement of the wrong facets of their existence.

Henri de Toulouse-Lautrec is the victim of café journalism and the warping of lurid events which have obscured the vital revolution he created in the modern poster and print. As an artist he was neither a freak nor a crackpot. The fact that he broke both his thigh bones at an early age and later broke them again, causing his legs to stop growing, was not such an unmixed disaster. Spoiled for the hunt, he could pursue his desire to become an artist with the approval of his family—a profession they would have frowned on had he been able to grow tall enough to take his place as a French nobleman, head of a great and overbred house going a little insane with its ancient ideas of its own worth.

Henri was born in Albi, near Toulouse, in 1864. His father was Alphonse de Toulouse-Lautrec Monfa; his mother was Adèle Tapié de Céleyran. The family traced itself carefully back to 1527, and the father most likely belonged behind restraining bars. He milked his riding mare in public and drank the result from a silver cup. He often wore armor, and he was the last medieval falconer in France.

The son was ugly, with thick lips, weak eyes hidden behind narrow pince-nez, and short, crippled legs. But in spirit and talent the boy was a giant. He began to study art with René Princeteau, a military and equestrian artist of fine talent. Lautrec, a skilled draftsman even in childhood, soon became a remarkable artist of the fashionable mode and proper horsemanship. His influences were the sour and dismal bigot Forain (who aped Daumier), Chavannes, Manet, Degas—and, above all, the Japanese woodcut prints for their color and pattern.

181. LAUTREC, Woman in Bed

Lautrec suggests to us in this print some sinister human drama, seen in the yellow gaslight of the 1890s and drawn in the clean, direct style of a child's fairy tale.
Lithograph, 15½" x 20⁷⁄₁₆", courtesy Museum of Modern Art, gift of Mrs. John D. Rockefeller, Jr.

180. LAUTREC, Woman Preparing Bathtub

Long before his paintings were accepted as important art, Lautrec was famous for his posters. Here he has carried over the folk art of the poster into an intimate household scene and created one of the most charming of his prints.

Lithograph, 15¹¹⁄₁₆″ x 20⅜″, courtesy Museum of Modern Art, gift of Mrs. John D. Rockefeller, Jr.

182.   LAUTREC, Mlle. Marcelle Lender

Lautrec's work, particularly his posters, reflects the influence of Japanese woodcut prints.
Here, the line and vision are the artist's own, yet how this portrait echoes the ironic mood
of the great actor prints by Sharaku, shown elsewhere in this book.

Lithograph, 21½" x 15⅝", courtesy of the Museum of Modern Art, gift of Mrs. John D. Rockefeller, Jr.

183. LAUTREC, Divan Japonais

With this poster Lautrec showed his disregard for the wall between folk art and fine art.
Designed to be pasted on a Paris street-corner wall, it differs in no way stylistically from
the many prints he made for collectors.

Lithograph, 31⅞″ x 24⁹⁄₁₆″, courtesy of the Museum of Modern Art, Mrs. John D. Rockefeller, Jr.,
Purchase Fund.

184. LAUTREC, Clown at the Moulin Rouge (Cha-U-Ka-O)

One of his most carefully made prints, it shows how technique can be harnessed to composition and balance established. Unlike Daumier, who makes masks of the characters in the human comedy, Lautrec exposes the features of his subjects to leave them naked but beyond shame.

Lithograph, 16″ x 12¾″, courtesy of the Museum of Modern Art, gift of Mrs. John D. Rockefeller, Jr.

Lautrec escaped from the society that Proust was soon to attempt to capture in his great work *À la Recherche du temps perdu,* escaped at a slow, crablike pace to Montmartre and its hills, to the artists and their models, the dance halls, sporting arenas, brothels and cafés. France was recovering from the great defeat at Sedan; the Third Republic was later to be buffeted about, dividing its citizens in the foul military perversion of the Dreyfus case. But Paris was a charming pleasure city, where Lautrec could live free of binding moral values and middle-class restrictions. He never preached, he never pitied himself. He wanted to seize life and impressions, see new beauty in the gutter, draw and paint and make his posters and prints.

In 1886 he met the half-mad visionary genius Vincent van Gogh and did a revealing pastel head of him. Lautrec was impressed and defended the red-bearded Dutchman. But he could not follow Vincent in his impassioned dedication to an ideal. Lautrec found his world dancing, drinking, fomenting little emotional plots and dramas àt the Cirque Fernando, Bruant's Cabaret Artistique, the Mirliton, and his favorites, the Moulin de la Galette and the Moulin Rouge. He was fascinated in the last place by a vulgar red-haired dancer of great skill and depraved vigor, La Goulue, and by her skinny, top-hatted dancing partner. In 1891 he incorporated the two of them into his first poster advertising the Moulin Rouge. It was a large colored lithograph print that made history. His posters soon covered Paris, and they were already being collected when no one paid much attention to his paintings and his print style was yet to be formed.

"The artist estranging himself from life becomes," Balzac had said, "the destroyer of his work." Lautrec was to destroy not his work but himself. He was always drawing, always filling little sketchbooks and bits of paper with a swift ironic line, a mocking, amusing way of seeing life swiftly and without blinders. Many of his subjects should repel us, but we accept his images of depraved girls, his intimate details of medical inspection of prostitutes, inverted men and women, the bedrooms of rakes and courtesans, because they neither preach nor snicker. The false sentiment of secondhand pity is missing, and so is the overripe seeking of mere sensation. What he put down in his drawings and in his prints is not the norm for most of society, but it is part of life and is keenly observed. His posters, in a remarkable shorthand, are an extension of his art, not the work of a hack or a cynical money-maker. He was the lucky artist with a private income.

TOULOUSE-LAUTREC

185. LAUTREC, The Costume Ball at the Moulin Rouge

Lautrec was one of the first to eliminate unnecessary detail and inject his own sense of satire. Here he uses white space to emphasize the images of vice at play.

Lithograph, 11 1/16" x 18 1/8", courtesy of the Museum of Modern Art, gift of Mrs. John D. Rockefeller, Jr.

Each of his posters was an amazing work of art, an entirely new concept of the poster in color and movement, reminding one of the figure prints of the great Japanese masters Sharaku and Utamaro. The combination of red hair and green-white flesh in yellow gaslight was his favorite; he experimented in color lithography to achieve those tones which became his own. He did his first lithograph print of Jane Avril, who sang with a black cat in her arms; Degas commented approvingly, "Ah, now you have joined us." And Lautrec celebrated by inventing a new cocktail. He was already an alcoholic, driven, as many artists are who have a hint of the short life granted them, to nerve-tearing tensions in his effort to grasp all he could.

His work appears to have been done effortlessly with a fast and biting line, yet it was the result of long years at the drawing pad. His art captured without moral mottoes the various levels of society, a society like a mine of many tunnels that never meet, yet do form an over-all design. Lautrec caught what are called epiphanies—sudden moments of seeing into the divine or mysterious. He cut away the anecdote in his prints to unmask wriggling humanity. He followed Daumier in creating symbolic masks for public figures in his print series; *Elles*, for example, was a series that caught the essence of actors, music-hall singers, café entertainers. He filed their features down to the basic elements of singing, laughing, talking creatures. Lautrec's aesthetic angle remained Japanese; he loved to collect the ukiyoye prints and he often dressed up as a geisha at parties and carried his favorite Japanese doll. He was a great wit, well read, and aware that he was transforming pathological material into art.

Leaning on his cane, his black-corded pince-nez well polished, the bearded little face locked in mirth, he went on his nocturnal jaunts dragging himself along on tiny legs. If he dissipated, he always worked very hard as well. He was no taster of life interested merely in lazy loafing. He created a long series of famous poster prints, working with the printer closely as to color and register; he did series after series of lithograph prints and also tried dry-point etching. His work acquired incredible verve.

Lautrec found Yvette Guilbert an entertainer of strangely fascinating appearance with her long black gloves, orange hair, tilted nose and pouting mouth. He did sixteen lithographs of her that caused her to shout at him, *"Petit monstre!"* He drew Suzanne Valadon, a young model turned artist, mother of an infant to be called Maurice Utrillo. He watched top-hatted Englishmen court the café girls, the thrill seekers on the Butte, the habitués of the Café des Décadents. He did an amazing color lithograph of a woman clown, "Cha-U-Kau, Seated." He could go from the elegance and vivacity of the best society to the Buffalo cycle track and capture that vivid tension that replaces the need for happiness as the night grows longer.

Lautrec's favorite artists became El Greco, Cranach and Uccello. His mind wandered and his health broke down. His eccentricities became those of a very sick man, and his mother had him committed to

TOULOUSE-LAUTREC

186. LAUTREC, Woman in a Corset

In Lautrec's lifetime, the artist was still to some degree the historian of society. This print, in both content and style, brings to life a mood of the period with the vividness of a page from Proust.

Lithograph printed in color, 20″ x 15½″, courtesy of the Museum of Modern Art, gift of Mrs. John D. Rockefeller, Jr.

187. LAUTREC, At the Moulin Rouge: La Goulue and Her Sister

In this print, the solid realism of the old masters is replaced with new methods of telling a story. The artist trims off the figures and the setting in dramatic ways in order to bring us closer to his purpose.

Lithograph printed in color, 18 1/16" x 13 9/16", courtesy of the Museum of Modern Art, gift of Mrs. John D. Rockefeller, Jr.

188. LAUTREC, Yvette Guilbert

The artist was the Homer of the Parisian theater world and café life. This portrait of a famous singer expresses a personal statement by Lautrec on that world and the people who lived in it.

Transfer lithograph, 11½" x 9⁹⁄₁₆", courtesy of the Museum of Modern Art, gift of Mrs. John D. Rockefeller, Jr.

189.   LAUTREC, The Jockey

Lautrec could make no statement that was not related to his own way of life. Even his horses are seen in a special light. They have the heads of snakes and the sleek grace of dancers at the Moulin Rouge.

Lithograph, 20⁷⁄₁₆″ x 14⅜″, courtesy of the Museum of Modern Art, gift of Mrs. John D. Rockefeller, Jr.

a sanatorium for alcoholics. To prove his sanity, he drew from memory a remarkable series of pastels, *The Circus*. He wrote to his father, pleading, "I am shut up, and everything that is shut up dies."

It was not his father but the series of circus pastels that set him free; they were not, the doctors agreed, the work of a man who had lost his mind. But the end was near. He traveled with a male nurse who was supposed to keep him from drink but failed. Lautrec drank, painted, prepared prints and then, in final collapse, went to his mother and sank deeper and deeper into indifference to all the pleasures and the problems of this world. His father fussed around the bed and Lautrec smiled and said, "The old bastard." It was 1901 when he died, at the age of thirty-seven. He had read Comenius: "Death is the last line written by life, so if the end be good, then all is good."

Lautrec's eyes opened modern art to the new print makers. His methods and styles were to set other young men to remodeling the art of the print. A hot-eyed young Spaniard in Paris was to begin by working in Lautrec's style. Picasso made no bones about what he had learned from the little nobleman. Rouault in his early work—his best—was to borrow much. Lautrec had established the validity of an epoch's living its own life as subject matter. He used the themes of the *fin de siècle* to create material for museum walls. His salvation was his love of the human spirit tinged with admiration for its form, no matter what its condition or how deep its degradation.

TOULOUSE-LAUTREC

THE HISTORIAN GIBBON gave it as his firm opinion: "The various modes of worship which prevailed in the Roman world were all considered by the people as equally true, by the philosopher as equally false, and by the magistrate as equally useful." So, to many, the various forms of modern art are considered by the enlightened people as equally true, by certain informed art philosophers as equally false, and by the critics and the museum magistrates as equally useful. Only Matisse could dare declare, "Art should be enjoyed like a comfortable chair." But that this is not his full philosophy on art is shown when he confesses, "The artist paints the best of himself into his pictures; what the artist says does not really matter."

His work is an antidote to troubled times, with its dreamy visions of odalisques waiting in pink languor behind blue wooden blinds, the lithographs of intimate flesh that are a sensibility of thickening and thinning lines, his images of tranquil vegetation—the souls of dahlias and pomegranates ("My curves do not run wild"). It is as a pantheist of joy uninhibited that he rebuilt the world.

Henri Émile Benoît Matisse was born in 1869 at Chateau Cambrésis. In 1887 he was—more or less seriously—at the University of Paris studying law. A few years later, convalescing from appendicitis, he copied some landscapes to amuse himself. It was not until 1891, when he was over twenty, that he enrolled in the Académie Julien, under Bouguereau and Ferris. It was late in life for a French artist to begin, but Matisse so impressed Gustave Moreau, the great teacher, that he was invited to his studio. Here one of his classmates was Rouault. They copied paintings at the Louvre, and in 1896 Matisse was still so close to respectable Academy style that his "Woman Reading" was bought by the state at the Salon de la Société Nationale.

Somewhere the artist had acquired a daughter, a sad child who, after an operation, breathed through a silver tube in her throat. When Matisse married Amélie Parayre, the girl joined the ménage. Times were hard, but the couple went to London for a honeymoon; there Matisse studied the last great paintings of Turner which hinted at the

Matisse

FRENCH
1869 - 1954

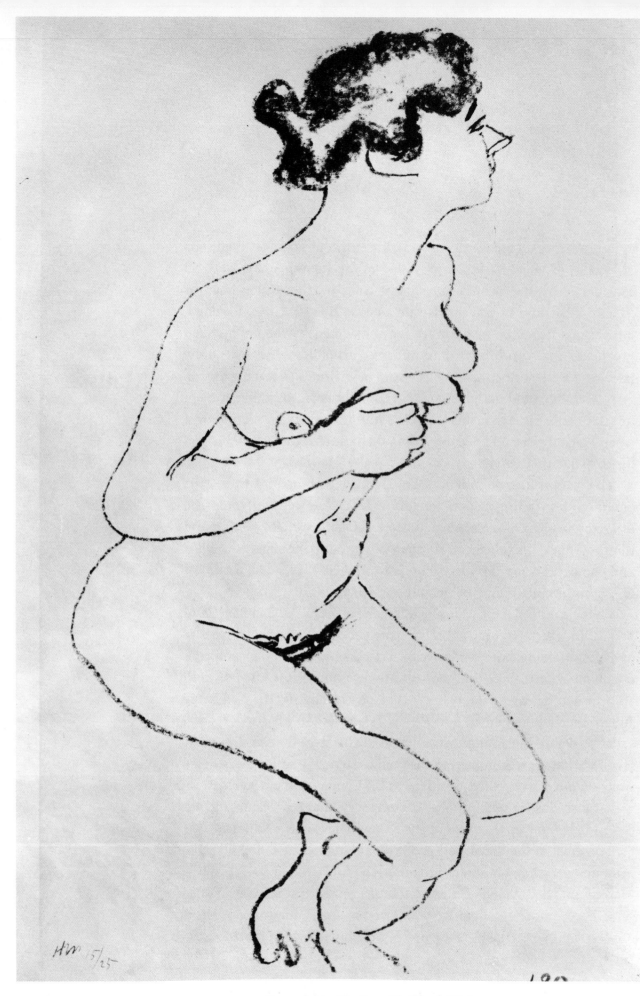

190.   MATISSE, Crouching Nude with Black Hair

The artist is creating directly from the subject, almost without looking at his work. It is the image of the instant that he wants to catch in this print, and he will distort rather than break his line.

Lithograph, 16⅝″ x 8¾″, courtesy of the Museum of Modern Art, Larry Aldrich Fund.

191. MATISSE, Nude Study

Made like a woodcut, this is an early example of Matisse's interest in the pattern of lines, of white against black, of moods created boldly with ink on paper. There is nothing to suggest that the artist wishes us to think this is real flesh.

Linoleum cut, 18¾″ x 15″, courtesy of the Museum of Modern Art, gift of Mr. and Mrs. R. Kirk Askew, Jr.

postimpressionism and expressionism of the future. Out of a skimpy income he bought from the dealer Vollard a small Cézanne, "Three Bathers."

All this led to financial difficulties, and Mme. Matisse opened a millinery shop on the Rue de Châteaudun. There are stories of Matisse painting expensive fruit in rooms kept icy cold to preserve the subject, and everyone eying it hungrily in the hope that it could be eaten before it spoiled.

In 1905 Matisse, with a wild explosion of color and form, was exhibiting at the Salon d'Automne as one of the group that became known as the Fauves (Wild Beasts). Leo Stein, brother of the opaque Gertrude, bought one of his paintings, and the Steins made a small vogue for Matisse. The next year Matisse began his long career in print making, doing his first lithographs and woodcuts. Soon he was being exhibited in New York and Moscow. A stuttering, shy little millionaire tea merchant, Sergei Shchukin, was to build up the first great Russian collection of Matisses, now one of the glories of a Soviet museum. In 1914 Matisse's pictures on exhibit in Berlin were seized by the Germans as enemy property.

MATISSE

His prints were like his paintings: self-control enhanced by vivacity and skill. When he took up the etcher's needle he was able to produce the purest emotions in bare line. His work progressed at high speed and we see in his many prints how he invents rhythms irrelevant to the objects, just for pure design. Matisse wanted no finished or exact reproduction of nature, of woman or of fruit. He stripped the subject naked, down to its basic form, and with a majestic ease and grandeur he instantaneously recorded it. It became again structurally solid, but with new wit and subtlety. His work was a kind of aesthetic shorthand that he invented to capture the tumbling nudes, the views of palms and skies, the small, intimate rooms hung with exotic rugs. Matisse worked with both freshness and a keen architectural order in his prints. Even Picasso seems like posed theater after examining one of Matisse's swift, novel impressions.

There was, as he grew older, an Orientalizing of form, and, as the great early critic of the period, Apollinaire, adds, "an order of which instinct sets the measure." Matisse needed sunlight and color, primitive form. He had already visited Corsica, Andalusia, Tangier; in 1930, already old and famous, he visited Tahiti. It was no ultimate holy goal, as it had been for Gauguin, but just a place to rearrange nature again. The next year the artist did a remarkable set of etchings for Skira's edition of Mallarmé's poems.

By 1938 Matisse had a sun-filled apartment in the former Hotel Régine at Cimiez above Nice, working on his subjects: girls, doves and blue-skied backgrounds. In the '40s he illustrated *The Amours of Ronsard* and Montherlant's *Pasiphaé*. He was separated from Mme. Matisse, a son Paul was an international art dealer, and the artist himself was mortally ill. He had a serious operation for an intestinal occlu-

192.   MATISSE, Girl with a Vase of Flowers

Neither realism nor photography could create the mood of this print. The artist asks us to accept an image which is more lush, more sensual, than the actuality from which he worked.

Lithograph, 10⅞″ x 7½″, courtesy of the Museum of Modern Art, gift of Mrs. John D. Rockefeller, Jr.

sion in a Lyons clinic. Often sick in bed, Matisse continued to draw with colored chalk at the end of a stick. He lost none of his power, but attended more to random ideas of beauty. "I never draw a curve," he said, "without bearing in mind its relation to the vertical." The poetic luminosity of atmosphere, the subtle nuances of a not-so-innocent line continued to mark his work. The apartment was always full of models, and the drawings and paintings piled up. In cut paper Matisse explored the inner secrets of décor. With daring foreshortening, he pictured the girls in what came to be known as Matisse poses. "The condensations of sensations," he called these languorous, swaying figures. Like a sultan cushioned among his harem beauties, Matisse worked on; his patterns had an austerity and dignity offset by playfulness, an intensive scrutiny crossed with grace. He grasped the exact limits of simplicity with his infallible line. "All that is not useful in a picture is harmful; rules have no existence outside of individuals."

MATISSE

Matisse moved to the villa Le Rêve at Vence. He was made a Commander of the Legion of Honor. To thank the nuns of the Dominican order at Vence, who had nursed him in his illness, he designed and decorated a chapel that was erected there. The old freethinker, the unbeliever, did it as a labor of love. It is beautiful, but like a theater lobby rather than a church; he lacked pious emotion.

The Berggruen Gallery in Paris held large shows of his graphic art and his lithographs in the early '50s. He lived on, an old sick man with a white beard, the models, the cut paper, the chalk at the end of the stick. In 1954 he died and was buried in the Cimiez cemetery, in ground given by the city of Nice.

"My life's long labor has been directed to the service of the great human family, which needs to be given glimpses of the unfading beauty of the world," he had written. His cadences of definitive forms are universal. He was one of those people who enjoy things with their skin, and he was aware that art is above nationality. An ironic artist sitting in a wheelchair at a window, he could enjoy the poet's lovely line, "God sends rain to sell umbrellas."

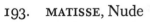

193. MATISSE, Nude

Freshness is all-important to the artist in this print. He has discarded the skillful tricks that once embellished an image. Here we feel the presence of complete, immediate reality.

Lithograph, 19¾" x 12", courtesy of the Museum of Modern Art, Frank Crowninshield Fund.

194. MATISSE, Arabesque

The artist had no great range of subject matter but a world of styles, all of which served to say something in a simple, yet new, way. Every part of this print has power and claims attention.

Lithograph, 19¹⁄₁₆″ x 12⅝″, courtesy of the Museum of Modern Art, Lillie P. Bliss Collection.

195. MATISSE, Odalisque in a Tulle Skirt

Matisse has not been afraid to use modeling here to round out his composition in the usual way. It is as if he were daring a conventional style to defeat him.

Lithograph, 11¼″ x 15″, courtesy of the Museum of Modern Art, gift of M. Knoedler and Co., Inc.

196. MATISSE, The Blinding of Polyphemus

This print at first appears to have been created by a few casual strokes suggesting the theme. Yet detailed drawings exist to show with what care the artist worked out the design before reducing it to this simplicity. Polyphemus was the Cyclops leader whom Odysseus blinded in order to escape him.

Soft ground etching for James Joyce's *Ulysses*, 11⅝" x 8⅞", courtesy Museum of Modern Art.

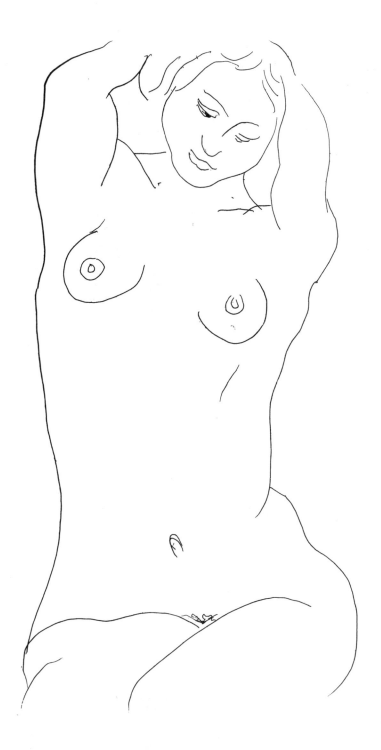

197. MATISSE, Nude, Arms Clasped over Head

Matisse's nudes are more than startling and original. Free of cloying detail, they express a pagan delight in the sensual world. His magic lay in creating the feel of living flesh with a few simple lines on paper.

Etching, 7¹⁄₁₆″ x 5″, courtesy of the Museum of Modern Art, Purchase Fund.

198.   MATISSE, Charles Baudelaire
(from Mallarmé's *Poésies*, 1932)

*A print of the great poet that differs from accepted portraits of the past. It
is as stark and immediate as a motion-picture closeup.*

Etching, 12″ x 9″, courtesy of the Museum of Modern Art, Mrs. John D. Rockefeller, Jr., Purchase Fund.

199. MATISSE, from *Anthology
of the Amours of Ronsard* (1941)

*Matisse, even at his most modern, is never merely fashionable. This
grouping will not date. Original as the drawings in this series are, they
state the theme simply and directly.*

Color lithograph, 15⅛″ x 11″, courtesy Museum of Modern Art, Purchase Fund.

Rouault

FRENCH
1871 - 1958

IN 1871 Paris was under siege again, not from the Germans this time, for the French had lost the war against Bismarck. The city was being held by the Commune, the people of the streets, against the attacks of the Versaillais, the extreme opposition party. Georges Rouault was born during this siege, and his first weeks on earth were lived during the great terror when thousands of Parisians were sent before the firing squads, Frenchmen killing Frenchmen, in the terrible vengeance of the Versaillais who had lost Sedan and the Second Empire.

Rouault grew up under the fond eyes of a grandfather who owned and collected prints by Callot, Rembrandt and Daumier. The old man and the boy used to haunt the print shops, hunting for their favorites. "I first went to the school of Daumier," he said later. At fourteen he was apprenticed to the stained-glass maker Hirsch. The boy's job was to sort out and fire bits of colored glass for the repair of church windows, separating the smoldering ruby-red glass from the electric blue-greens and setting in place the heavy black lead contours that delineated angels' wings and the holy saints and martyrs. The boy was happy among the Gothic intensity of old art. Years later he admitted, "My real life is back in the age of the cathedrals."

When sent on errands, he went afoot and saved the omnibus fare to buy drawing paper. He attended night classes at the École Nationale des Arts Décoratifs, and in 1891 he was in the École des Beaux-Arts. Here he was the favorite pupil of the painter Gustave Moreau, a good artist but better known as a fine teacher.

Rouault learned to sum up a painting or a print by a few essential traits. As he expressed it later, "Art is the furious tracking down of the inner feeling." His earlier work was also done in the pursuit of serious subject matter. Many critics feel this is his best work, these early butchers, prostitutes, clowns, the destitute living under bridges, the coarse faces of sinners, all the symbols of decay and earthly degradation. The line is black and thick, like the lead contours in the stained-glass windows; the forms are taken over from Daumier and Lautrec, yet added are personal details. The images are the grimaces of a fleshly martyrdom.

"An outrageous lyricism," the artist calls these stark, brutal forms, these huge *filles de joie* with no joy in their work. The streak of revolting sensuality is almost pathological. Rouault's work of this period has never been fully studied by the art historians. It was more than a hunt for powerful forms, for sinners to redeem.

In 1902 Rouault helped to found the Salon d'Automne. He had become a kind of religious fanatic; he feared the free-wheeling intellectuals and called them victims of "cerebral morphiomania." By 1905 most of the ferocity and power of his early work was gone, and he was to adopt a more spiritual and settled approach to life and art. Jacques Maritain, the Catholic writer and his friend, said, "He belongs to the category of the shy explosions." Religious writers were his closest friends, his guides to subject matter. He began to work more in New Testament themes, and in Greek mythology as used by his master, Gustave Moreau. There are fine self-portraits and much drawing of sin and redemption, and his work, while not yet famous, was becoming known. He belonged to the Fauve generation of 1905, but was never part of it. He exhibited with Druet in Paris in 1910 and again in 1911.

During World War I Rouault began to collect the material for his greatest prints, the series now known as *Miserere et Guerre*. They were commissioned by the dealer-publisher Vollard and started in 1916, but it was not until 1948 that the great series of prints was issued, by L'Étoile Filante in Paris, in 450 sets. They are the most amazingly evolved prints of the twentieth century, the result of bold experimentation. From his drawings the artist made gouache and oil paintings, and these were photoengraved onto 18-by-21-inch copper plates. Rouault reworked these plates for years by hand, with aquatint, dry point, roulette, and even brush painting in acid on the copper. Often he took fifteen successive states of a plate before he felt it was right.

It is a powerful series, drawing upon one artist's integrity and sorrow for its subject matter. Man's fate on earth is pictured in forms that are based on stained-glass art and Daumier, but are at times almost as simple as a child's drawing on a wall. These are serious dramas of a Grand Guignol world, a theater of horror, of death and skeletons, redeemed by the artist's faith in a spiritual order of things. They are almost messages preaching that one must renounce the

200. ROUAULT, Know ye that so many of us as were baptized into Jesus Christ
were baptized into His death

*Everything is drawn with one line; surface communication is direct and stark. There is no
color, no beauty of form to delight us. It is a moment that calls for serious attention.*

Aquatint and drypoint over heliogravure, 21⅝" x 16⅝", courtesy of the Museum of Modern Art,
Mrs. John D. Rockefeller, Jr., Purchase Fund.

world, for it can never be fully possessed. They insist that in the inner citadel of the spirit sits the one answer: the soul.

Rouault was an enigma and remained one to the art world and even to himself. Small, almost wispy, given to wearing a surgeon's white gown and an operating-room cap, he was aware of publicity and knew the value of his public image. He could sue an art dealer for the return of 803 paintings, claiming they were unfinished or not up to his standard, then publicly announce that most would be burned and pose in front of a furnace tossing something into the fire; yet it is doubtful if the frugal Frenchman that lived inside him actually destroyed much of value.

He worked like a mole, in semisecrecy, keeping his prints and paintings close to him for years. He saw that the fluctuating phases of a picture are like an interminable drama; all of its complex movement must be clarified, like a love affair, through quarrel and reconciliation, hope and disillusion, jealousy and remorse. And yet at times an ironical detachment overtook him, and he reduced everything to a few brutal, direct lines. He saw that, like the love affair, once a picture is done it is ended, finished; the true ecstatic glow cannot be recaptured by the mind and body—the afterstare of analysis cannot revive the original passion of a moment. So Rouault kept his work around him, promising and not delivering, finding faults, tormenting those who had to work with him, and always trying to edge closer to the direct and final statement.

For him, unlike many modern artists, the past did not dissolve absolutely; it remained, in little pockets of memory. He accepted the facts of the external world, but brooded while his vision was being transformed into new intellectual and emotional equivalents of lost sensations. It was hard to give up the bodies of the whores, the gross faces of judges, the meanness of the market place, and settle for imagined saints and the Christ. He had hoped once for a lovelier and more lasting reality. He had learned differently.

For Rouault the creator of art is hemmed in by life; it hammers on his senses, his imagination, his sensibility. He sees what he suspects is the truth, but keeps some of his illusions, an appreciation that is sadly romantic. Rouault's secret was that he began life as a romantic and fought this all his years as an artist. Disillusionment only added to the spectacle of a full and spinning world which he tried to hold up to some moral judgment.

ROUAULT

Essai cuivre Miserere . Premier essai —   Dame du Haut Quartier   [9ème] Georges Rouault

201. ROUAULT, The society lady fancies she has a reserved seat in heaven

This almost seems to be a spontaneous visualization dashed off in dislike and at great speed. Yet the artist worked for months, even years, on these copper plates, in order to produce such eloquent silhouettes.

Aquatint, drypoint and roulette over heliogravure, 22⅞" x 16⅜", courtesy of the Museum of Modern Art, gift of the artist.

202.   ROUAULT, We think ourselves kings

We see here the debt Rouault owed to Daumier. But gone is Daumier's delight in bone and muscle, in kinship with a crowded world. The mask has lost all humanness, and dementia has taken over.

Aquatint and roulette over heliogravure, 23¾₁₆″ x 16⅝″, courtesy of the Museum of Modern Art, gift of Samuel A. Berger.

203.   ROUAULT, Love ye one another

Everything is line here. Cryptic stylization takes the place of anatomy, of feature and expression. It is another kind of shorthand.

Aquatint and drypoint over heliogravure, 23⅜″ x 16¾″, courtesy of the Museum of Modern Art, Mrs. John D. Rockefeller, Jr., Purchase Fund.

204. ROUAULT, The law is hard, but it is the law

It is easy to guess from this print that the artist once worked with the black strips of lead that separate stained-glass pictures. A strong, extreme style is used to create the image of a formidable personality.

Etching, aquatint, drypoint and roulette over heliogravure, 22⁹⁄₁₆″ x 17¼″, courtesy of the Museum of Modern Art, gift of the artist.

205.   ROUAULT, Sometimes the blind have comforted those who can see

In most of the prints reproduced here the artist has photographed paintings on copper, then engraved and etched on the metal until very little of the original painting was left. Here, external appearances are transfixed, and the unconscious waits just under the surface to startle us.

Etching, aquatint and heliogravure, 23″ x 17⅛″, courtesy of the Brooklyn Museum.

206.   ROUAULT, Obedient unto death, even the death of the cross

This is no Nordic athlete balanced with grace on a cross of high-quality wood. Rouault has returned to the tormented Jew, neither pretty nor joyous in his final moment.

Aquatint, drypoint and roulette over heliogravure, 23$\frac{1}{16}$″ x 16$\frac{11}{16}$″, courtesy of the Museum of Modern Art, Mrs. John D. Rockefeller, Jr., Purchase Fund.

He turned to poetry to better examine himself and his world.

"Tomorrow will be beautiful," said the shipwrecked man
Just before he sank beneath the gray horizon.

Peace seems never to rule
Over this world in agony
Made of shams and shadows.

Jesus tells you this on the Cross
Better than I can.

ROUAULT

Rouault was one of the few who understood that one must often give up an immediate desire to achieve a future goal. His awe of God made him, in the end, approach life from a moral angle. Out of the welter of experiences, he was forming an absolute world. His images became the product of a mind involved in an austere attack on evil, an attack with a vocabulary of a rediscovered artistic syntax: faith.

The critics began to make strange remarks about his stark, simple style. "Rouault is not above painting in slang," said one. And of his prints during the '20s another said, "Ferocity here knows how to laugh."

He published his poems *Paysages légendaires* with his own illustrations in 1929, showing that inside the artist was not only the brooding darkness of bitter mysticism but a desire for elegant living, for the world of *le Roi Soleil*, for the splendor of Versailles. It is no shock to discover that a follower of the Church was also a royalist; for a time the idea of the *fêtes galantes* replaced his nightmares of the *maisons closes*.

The series *Miserere* is the high tide of the artist's work. The later work, still masterful, is often banal, and the repeating of the same themes begins to cloy; the blank white faces of clowns, the candy-box Christs show that even a master can become trapped in over-pictorial expression. There is too much of the personality and even the prejudices of the artist in this work. Flaubert had been right when he said, "The artist, like God, should always be present, but never visible."

He died in 1958 and by government decree was given a state funeral. He was eighty-six. Near the end he had written:

Of all criticisms, of judgments more or less enlightened, biased or

207.　ROUAULT, My sweet homeland, what has become of you?

The world burns and people watch, helpless to change their condition. This is a polemic and an allegorical piece in which Rouault tries to strip everything down to a child's drawing of tragic awe.

Etching, aquatint, drypoint and roulette over heliogravure, 16¹¹/₁₆″ x 23⁹/₁₆″, courtesy of the Museum of Modern Art, gift of the artist.

rash, of all miseries and vanities of the moment, there remains a mute though sometimes eloquent witness. I mean the poor fragment of canvas or paper before which our contemporaries and those to follow will sing "Hallelujah" or "Miserere," sometimes without having any idea of the conditions under which the creator may have been constrained to work.

208.   ROUAULT, War, which all mothers hate

The fleshy studio models of high Italian art are gone. This is like an early icon-painting, where mother and child form a design that the simplest soul can understand.

Etching, aquatint, drypoint and roulette over heliogravure, 23″ x 17⅞″, courtesy of the Museum of Modern Art, gift of the artist.

209. ROUAULT, This will be the last time, little father!

Like Goya, like Daumier, the artist mocked the slogans that say the current war is always the last one, fought for some noble phrase. The men of both armies are assured that God is on their side. Rouault balances a difficult composition with great skill.

Aquatint, drypoint and roulette over heliogravure, 23⅜″ x 17″, courtesy of the Museum of Modern Art, gift of the artist.

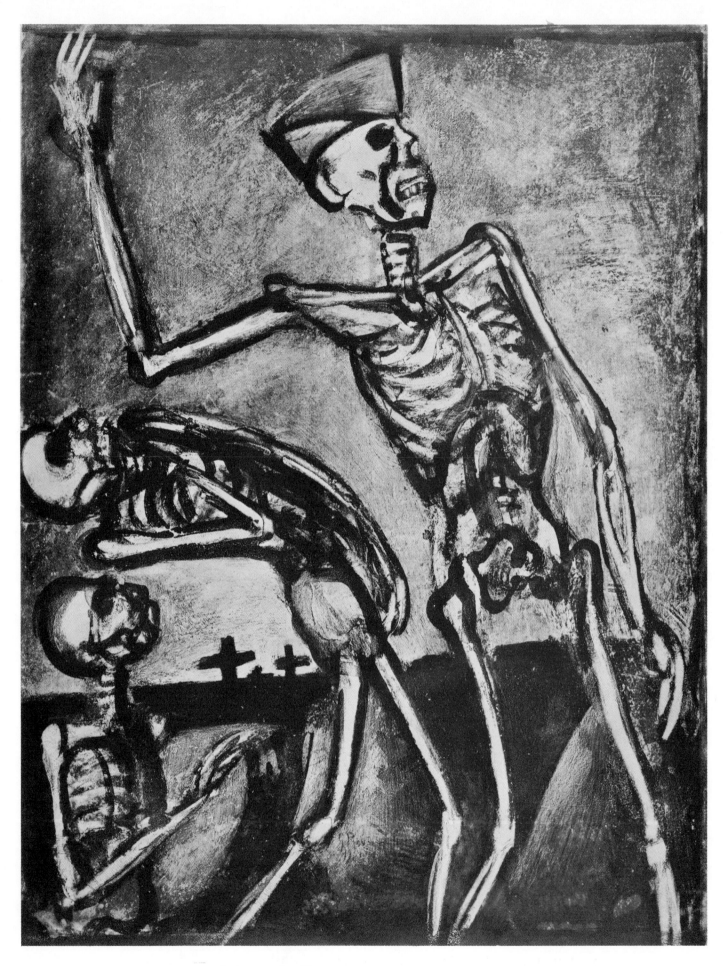

210.   ROUAULT, Arise, ye dead!

Death is not real here; it is a calligraphy of old bones. Rouault's soldiers arise from their graves in the trenches to perform a grim ballet. The print expresses the artist's feeling for the reality of Judgment Day.

Aquatint, drypoint, and roulette over heliogravure, 23⅛″ x 17½″, courtesy of the Museum of Modern Art, gift of the artist.

211. ROUAULT, The Prostitute

A gross body and emotional instability are reproduced in subtle, iridescent grays and poignant blacks. This is not desire or lust, but the sad ineptitude of a society that hides its vices.
Lithograph, 12⅞" x 9", courtesy of the Museum of Modern Art, gift of Mrs. John D. Rockefeller, Jr.

212.   ROUAULT, Flotsam

There is no detail, no sharpness in this print. The artist sees his subjects as obscure figures in the social pattern. They are reduced to dim impressions, yet remain powerful enough to move us.

Lithograph, 11⅞″ x 8⅜″, courtesy of the Museum of Modern Art.

213. ROUAULT, Self-portrait

Rouault exposes only half his face. There is a double identity: the clown and the would-be saint. Melancholy lurks among the dark shadows. Yet the air of taciturn modesty is deceptive.

Color lithograph, 13⅝" x 9⅞", courtesy of the Museum of Modern Art, gift of Mrs. John D. Rockefeller, Jr.

214. ROUAULT, Portrait of a Man

The antithesis of fashionable portrait styles. Wearing an Iron Cross, this old man could be Von Hindenberg preaching German dreams of power. Christ becomes a mere gesture, a bit of wall décor—or perhaps an ironic comment—in such a setting.

Aquatint, 24″ x 17⅝″, courtesy of the Museum of Modern Art.

PABLO PICASSO has spent his whole life hunting for the mystic center of experience. He has tried to penetrate Bergson's time and consciousness of reality. To some his work is an example of the great search: what we are we become only in time and through time. His dealer Daniel Kahnweiler has said, "With Picasso, art . . . is a confession to mankind."

Picasso was born into mankind at Málaga, at the extreme southern tip of the Iberian Peninsula. His father was José Ruiz Blasco, a painter of bird life, a teacher of talentless young artists. His mother came from a family of silversmiths from Majorca. The father was a disappointed man who saw other less talented men achieve fame. His young dark-eyed son, short, strong and black-haired, was soon helping him with his bird paintings. Picasso as a boy studied at the Academy of Fine Arts, Barcelona, and at the Royal Academy of San Fernando in Madrid, schools that had long since lost any of the vitality that El Greco and Goya had painted into Spanish life. The father gave up painting when his son showed himself a remarkable child artist. Soon the teen-age artist was making drawings for the local *art-nouveau* journals, sitting in at the café bull sessions where art enthusiasts talked of Paris and the exciting work of Toulouse-Lautrec. It was lively talk. Picasso was already resourceful, intense. He did his first etching, of which only one copy has survived—"El Zurdo (The Left-handed Man)," a portrait of a seated picador from the bull ring. It is signed "P. Ruiz Picasso" and also contains a sketch of an owl, a bird that still appears in some of the work of the great artist in his old age.

By 1900 Picasso had been to Paris, felt the excitement there, seen the new art forms and starved; one freezing winter night he fed the studio stove with piles of his drawings and sketches to keep warm. By 1904 he was settled in Montmartre, at the Rue Ravignan studio building called the Bateau-Lavoir—the Laundry Boat.

But he always remained a Spaniard in love with his Mediterranean memories: sea gulls, small and white as doves, the legends of Peje Nicolao (who was half fish, half man), the smoking suckling pig, the

Picasso

SPANISH
1881 -

215. PICASSO, The Frugal Repast

Almost a parody of styles—Daumier's subject matter, El Greco's elongated figures and fingers. We are held by the mystery of lonely lovers, each in the shadow of his own world; by the dry thinness of their mood.

Etching, 18³⁄₁₆″ x 14¹³⁄₁₆″, courtesy of the Museum of Modern Art, gift of Mrs. John D. Rockefeller, Jr.

revolutionary song "Los Segadores." He was Spanish in his blood, and his face suggested the Phoenician history of Mare Nostrum, Our Sea, where he had played naked on the white sands as a small boy and eaten from the family pot of cod and rice. He was to become the leader of the school of Paris, but it did not ever make him fully French. In his drawings he returned to the world of his daydreams, the great cuttlefish and octopuses of the Spanish markets, and he saw back to the days of Rome and Greece with the harbor talk of the still-present wrecks of the Liburnian feluccas and Carthaginian biremes that fouled the fishing nets.

Picasso also remembered warmly the days of the *corrida,* the bulls moving from the station to the bull ring in saffron-colored dust; he read the bullfight papers *La libertad* and *El eco taurino.* Seated at the *barrera,* he would watch a young fighter work out *rodillazos* with his cape. Later he painted these things, drew them, etched them, when he was lonely for Spain, a Spain he could not live in, for it had become on the official salon level a land of false sentiment. And about sentiment Picasso was to agree with D. H. Lawrence:

PICASSO

> Sentimentalism is the working off on yourself of feelings you haven't really got. We all want to have certain feelings: feelings of love, of passionate sex, of kindliness, and so forth. Very few people really feel love, or sex passion, or kindliness, or anything else that goes at all deep. So the mass just fake these feelings inside themselves. Faked feelings! The world is all gummy with them. They are better than real feelings, because you can spit them out when you brush your teeth; and then tomorrow you can fake them afresh.

Picasso settled permanently in Paris the year of his first important etching, "The Frugal Repast," two thin, hungry lovers staring at an empty table. It might well be a picture of Picasso and his girl friend, La Belle Fernanda. All his life Picasso was to be involved with women, to paint them and to love them. But art was paramount. He studied new forms with Braque, from Negro and folk art, and later with Juan Gris and Léger. He etched Salome and circus folk and began to shape the world into cubism—geometry waylaying nature, art taking on analytical forms beyond the normal eye and orchestrated by genius. By the time the outer world was sunk in trench warfare in 1914, Picasso had begun his own journeys to the wars, the outer reaches of art never before visited.

The war killed his good friend, the fat critic and poet Guillaume

216. PICASSO, Mother Combing Her Hair

There are no extra lines in this print of a poor circus family. In the drawing is the meagerness of poverty, but not of the artist's imagination. Neither color nor shading would add to the skill and charm of this etching.

Etching on zinc, 9¼″ x 7″, courtesy of the Museum of Modern Art, gift of Mrs. John D. Rockefeller, Jr.

217. PICASSO, Still Life with Bottle

The line and scratch are all; it is the placing of these marks that makes the picture. The result is a print both daring and old-fashioned. On the one hand, it swings out in the manner of the cubists who shattered surfaces to find new forms. At the same time, the style is that of the conventional drypoint etching.

Drypoint etching, 19¹¹⁄₁₆″ x 12″, courtesy of the Museum of Modern Art, purchased through the Lillie P. Bliss Bequest.

218.   PICASSO, **Scul**ptor and Model

*Here the artist has adopted a pure line. Only in the face and upper torso of the girl has he
boldly, almost with a grin, shown us the formal way to suggest roundness.*
Etching, 14½″ x 11¹¹⁄₁₆″, courtesy of the Museum of Modern Art, Purchase Fund.

314

219. PICASSO, Minotauromachy

In one huge etching, Picasso combines the themes of his first great print-making period. He has gathered together the recurrent symbols that are enigmas even to him: the bull-headed man, the strange perverseness of budding girlhood, the philosopher climbing his ladder to no-goal logic. The result is one of the best prints of modern times.
Etching, 19½" x 27⅟₁₆", courtesy of the Museum of Modern Art, Purchase Fund.

Apollinaire, who was the first champion of cubism. In 1917 Picasso escaped the war by going to Rome with Jean Cocteau and Diaghilev, for whom he designed ballet sets and costumes. He also married a Russian ballet dancer and attempted to set up a middle-class domestic life with this dark woman from the north, who suspected all Latins were unworthy compared to Slavs. In 1919 he showed his first lithographs, and, as prosperity and a son came to the marriage, he bought a grand estate not far from Paris. He fitted out luxurious studios and had a chauffeur-driven Hispano. The dull tranquillity of contentment did not last for long.

It was a strange life for him, but he felt it was worth a try as he cut cubistic prints on a copper plate with a burin, made clown drawings, still-life compositions, portraits of Mme. Picasso, his friend Max Jacob and others. His sensitive use of dry-point etching was amazing. He drew women bathing, classic nudes of delicate poise that recalled Greek forms. He pulled prints of jugglers, saltimbanques, circus life. In the '20s he was back in Paris when it was being invaded by the "lost generation." Expatriates like the Steins took him up, and Picasso became as famous as a movie star.

In the 1920s Skira, the art publisher, commissioned him to illustrate Ovid's *Metamorphoses*, and Vollard to make plates for Balzac's *Le Chef-d'oeuvre Inconnu*. Picasso brought a new kind of line to drawing and etching in books, illustrating the powerful art of the past with his own delicate sweep in an economy of matter that told as much as the text.

From the first he poured his sympathy for human suffering into his lithographs, etchings and drawings. He had begun as a boy with a deep vein of wonder, a monumental energy that soon pulsated into a rushing drive to record and redesign life. Picasso was always in a contemplative ferment, trying to grab the essence of expression with his slim nudes, his thin girls—all in an aura of blue mystery that hung over his plates. Here was no Lautrec whispering as he died, "Life is a fine thing, they say." Picasso, for all his brooding, was a yea-sayer— he saw Shaw's Life Force at work, even in the vagrant existence of the *cirque forain*, in the emaciated harlequins, in the sad solitude of women with large-eyed hungry children.

At the beginning he was the painter of transient troubles and of shabby rooms, and over his work there hung a silence in which no one dared speak. In this early work who can imagine anyone saying a word? His line remained meticulous, sparse, hushed. Line was to be replaced by form, the subtle placidity of pattern expanded to become a new classicism. Now Picasso took up forms unlinked to visual references, things alien to popular design. He and his followers set off an architectural explosion with an analytical construction based on Negro or archaic Iberian style. "Les Demoiselles d'Avignon" (1907) summed up this new start; full of ritual and fetish, it had a purity of nonreasoning, a simplicity of symbolic structure.

He had discovered a shocking appeal as simple and nerve-tingling as Congo drums. His work was part of the breaking down of the

PICASSO

220. PICASSO, Weeping Woman

To express the horror of modern war, the artist has set out to redesign the human face.
This is a study for "Guernica," his tremendous protest against the bombing of men, women
and children by German planes flying under Franco during the Spanish Civil War.

Etching and aquatint, 27⅛" x 19⁷⁄₁₆", courtesy of the Museum of Modern Art, extended loan from
the artist.

221. PICASSO, The Cock

The accepted etching styles of "Minotauromachy" and "The Frugal Repast" are discarded. In every curl, the handwriting here is personal to the artist. Picasso dominates the copper plate, no longer using it in the demanding ways of his earlier etchings.

Aquatint, printed in black and gray, 10½″ x 8⅜″, courtesy of the Museum of Modern Art, gift of Mrs. John D. Rockefeller, Jr.

worn-out elements in art—the telling of new truths that hurt the eye of the beholder. Linear perspective had been discarded, cubism led to an alchemy of shards.

Picasso was never without a past. He had grasped, saluted and left behind El Greco, Goya, Poussin, Ingres, Corot, Cézanne, Seurat. Cylinders, cones, spheres, had their moment; geometry was truly a way of saying nature. In the middle '20s came the baroque arabesque of large brown women, a quest to recover the mother gods of Greek and Roman forms, and the booty of this new rape of the Sabines was organized in a new way. There appeared nymphs, Pans, naiads; creatures from forest and sea floated on his prints. Mask and features became mixed—a moment of idyllic serenity, and Picasso was off again to dissect the modern world with moving figures violently distorted and begging the artist for mercy. "Reason is no model," Ingres had said. "The artist who follows his ruler and compass follows a phantom." Picasso created his own anatomy of the human race, new kinds of twentieth-century bones.

Picasso's marriage was a failure, his moods of despair and loneliness came and went. For all that, he was the most talked-of artist in the world. He was fashionable, he was collected, he was mocked and called a fraud. Under the bang of black hair two very large dark eyes stared out at the world, and the well-muscled mouth tightened. He remade his forms of human bodies, fragments of bodies, of simultaneous impressions of moving figures all seen in one picture. He did the covers of the magazine *Minotaure*, and then he summed up all his print forms in one great etching, "Minotauromachy," a collection of his past and present, of myth and fact, of ritual and custom. The bull, the dead bullfighter, the two innocent little flower girls, the philosopher on the ladder to nowhere, the mocking wanton girls of the town, the doves, all were his own images, all were an enigma.

If he had his unhappy moments, so did the world of the '30s growing its bad seeds. The diabolical held Picasso; his work gave way to forms of tricky hallucinations; he went down into the rich cave of universal myth—bullheaded men, rapes, orgies in bay leaves. He redressed the old legends or reduced them to a few basic lines of etching or lithograph.

Then there came the disaster that was to produce a modern masterwork, a Great Wall. Spain, where his parents lived, was on fire. Franco and his Moors were cutting Christian throats, invaders joined

PICASSO

222. PICASSO, Young Boy

Picasso, like Shakespeare, is a great borrower. He has gone back to the classical style of wax paintings found on ancient Egyptian coffin lids to give us this haunting image of adolescence hovering between reality and vision.

Lithograph, 12¼″ x 9⅜″, courtesy of the Museum of Modern Art, Curt Valentin Bequest.

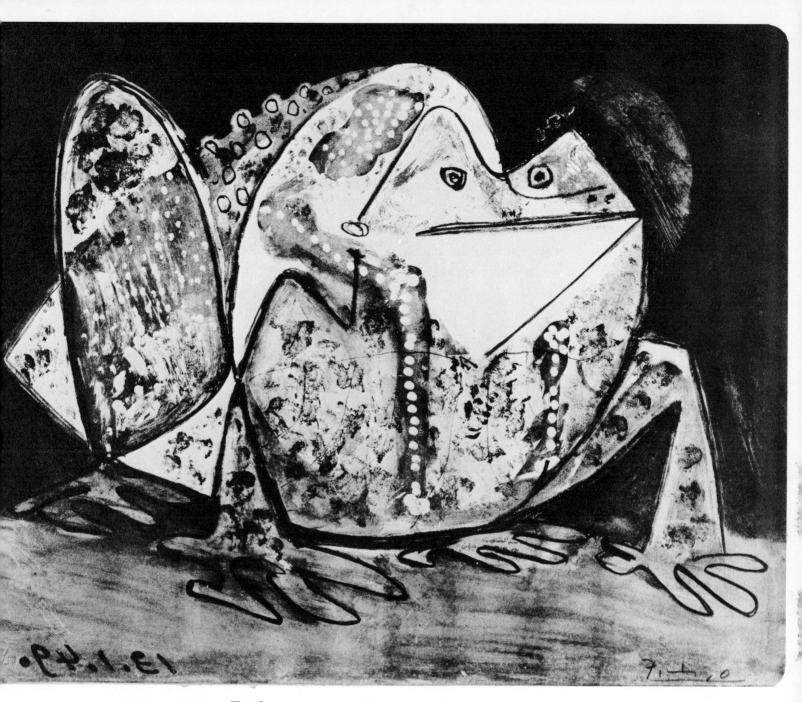

223.   PICASSO, Toad

In art that is original and great, the effects may seem easy, almost as simple as a child's work. Who would not delight in this toad? Yet all the tricks of lithography are added for enrichment.

Lithograph, 19⅝″ x 25¼″, courtesy of the Museum of Modern Art, Mrs. John D. Rockefeller, Jr., Purchase Fund.

both sides in civil war, and in his agony Picasso created "Guernica" using a new language. The cruelty, the darkness, the horror—Picasso could tell it all to modern man with only a bull, a stricken horse, a lamp, the limp corpse of a baby and a woman distorted to a scream by grief. He didn't even need color. The experiments of studio life had become a religion of forms.

He engraved it again on a series of plates he called *Sueño y Mentira de Franco* (*The Dream and the Lie of Franco*), small etchings racked with fury and pity. When the Germans came to Paris in 1941 and, in homage, asked, "Are you the one who made 'Guernica'?," he said, "No, *you* did."

Picasso gave thanks to Rembrandt by drawing etchings of the man at work; he did portraits of his print publisher Vollard; he printed thirty-one remarkable and novel plates for Buffon's *Histoires naturelles*.

He was getting old, the hair was going, many friends were dead, the past was gray and tasteless to him. He wanted youth, he wanted love. In the south of France, tanned by the sun, creating new forms, he made more prints, bucolic plates of fauns and nudes, and turned out dozens of lithograph stones marked *"Bon à tirer"* (ready to print).

Françoise Gilot, a young woman painter, became his companion; they had two children; he sketched them and went on drawing bulls and bullfights, pigeons too, for he loved the birds his father used to paint. But Françoise left him and took the children. To the press she said, "Who wants to live with a monument?" In 1961, he married Jacqueline Roque, with whom he lives in Provence.

And Picasso had become a monument, the most famous of living artists, the most praised, the most condemned. It didn't matter any more. He worked. He did prints of ideas based on Cranach's "David and Bathsheba," and a mockery of knights in armor like modern machines turned into weapons. If there were still those who could not explain him, they could read Nietzsche: "Truth has never yet hung on the rim of an absolute." The world was in a period without a style. He would give them a dozen to pick from. Our present is the result of the past, the Proustian novel tells us, so an artist can plunder history to come up with one original line. Tolstoy saw the times as the estrangement of art from the people for the few. The artist says, If only a few understand, there is hope.

With his first success Picasso had observed, "I could live well by just renting out the guitars in my still lifes to other artists." When someone objected to cubism, he quoted a philosopher: "If triangles ever had a religion, God would have three sides."

In old age he has worked on, saying that he has no time "to sit and wait for the bullet in the head—only the not completely achieved is life."

PICASSO

224. PICASSO, Seated Woman (after Cranach the Younger)

Picasso did a series of prints in the mood if not the style of various painters of the past. Cranach the Younger (his father is the better-known Cranach) was a 16th-century German artist who painted a number of portraits with the subject's hands crossed. Picasso has captured the repose of that position as well as the costume details of the time, transforming these elements into a work that is unmistakably his own.

Color linoleum cut, 25⅜″ x 21″, courtesy Museum of Modern Art, gift of Mrs. Daniel Saidenberg.

Chagall

RUSSIAN
1887

IN THE 1880s the city of Vitebsk, in czarist Russia, still looked like a tenth-century Byzantine town. It was raw, primitive, and the Jewish families who made up half its population of sixty thousand—large families ruled by patriarchs in beards and tallises (prayer shawls) —were primitives themselves. Marc Chagall was born there in 1887, the son of a man who worked for a herring dealer, herring being the still-life motif of the town. His mother ran a small store and had produced eight daughters and two sons. Their relatives were cattle dealers, fiddlers, barbers; the boy's grandfather, a tanner, hung animal hides around his house like drapes. Many of their people were of the Chasidic sect. The synagogue rituals and the high-holiday observances were the only forms of sport.

The boy began to draw when still young; he was taught a bit by a local painter and soon went to St. Petersburg, where he got into the school of the Society for the Protection of the Arts. Later Chagall was admitted into the studio of the theatrical designer Bakst and had his eyes opened to the fashionable forms then stirring up Paris. By 1908 he had adopted a wild, home-grown style, based on illogical fantasy and the new ideas. He transformed memory into visualizations of the sorrows, joys, processions and hungers of his native town. His work was a good tool for capturing the still-medieval Jews and their arks and Torahs, their weddings, their death watches, their daily work, onto canvas. He had a girl named Bella and was a young man on his way up.

By 1910 he was in Paris, wide-eyed, eager, in need of a haircut, moving with the postimpressionist tide and the cubistic adventurers. His best work is of this period, canvas after canvas of gay Yiddish forms in the best Paris styles, all tied together with a mystic verve, a kind of offering to the gods of his fathers, the sensual dreams of his love for Bella. His inner vision and the memory of the home town merged into forms outside time but inside a tribal culture soon to be dispersed by revolution and emigration.

He returned to Russia just in time to watch the Romanovs' nation commit suicide. In 1915 he was in an Army camouflage unit, marking war tools with the shapes of Picasso's and Braque's cubism. He was also married to Bella. His art retreated to the town, and he painted the rabbis in pre-Egyptian beards, the blue snow of winter, the miracles of fiddlers and candlesticks on rooftops, of lovers doing dream dances in the sky, defying gravity. Under Lenin and Trotsky he was appointed commissar of fine arts for the Vitebsk district, but his introduction of modern art forms failed to please the powers in control. Chagall's revolutions were all in form and not in politics—forms blithely floating, bizarrely balanced.

In 1922 Chagall and Bella were back in Paris, and his first period of print making began. Vollard got him to do eighty-five etchings for Gogol's great novel *Dead Souls*. Like most of Vollard's publishing ventures, they were late in seeing print; Chagall's illustrations for the book did not appear till 1948. The fables of La Fontaine attracted Chagall next; in his wispy, mystical style he did one hundred etchings that seem to be childishly simple and yet so philosophically true.

As the years passed, he continued to exploit the material of his youth in his painting, and while much of it was of high quality, his ideas began to repeat themselves; he turned out too much that was merely a restatement made for dealers and collectors. The youth, the vigor and the memory wore thin. Chagall was fashionable, and often empty. In 1941 he came to the United States. In 1944 Bella died. Returning, an old man, to France in 1949, he settled at Vence on the Côte d'Azur to repeat old formulas and to work on some very fine prints with Biblical themes. He has also continued to do decor and costume design. Of his stage props and images Chagall has said, "I don't understand them. They are only arrangements that obsess me."

An important artist, Chagall broke the laws of physics and made the mystical experience familiar. He helped father surrealism, and in his prints he stands as one of the best of modern artists, with a style so personal that one can almost imagine he had never seen other etchings, had only remembered old prayers: *Yhi shem adonai m'vorach me-ato v'ad olom.* May the name of the Lord be blessed from this time and forever.

225. CHAGALL, Cover for La Fontaine's *Fables*

In a fable, animals serve to teach or shame or amuse men. They act and talk like human beings. Here the artist keys his style to the mood of the fable. He is illustrating the story of the fox and the crow.

Etching, 15¼″ x 11¾″, courtesy of the Museum of Modern Art, Larry Aldrich Fund.

226. CHAGALL, La Fontaine's *Fables*: Cat Changed to a Woman

A man loved his cat so much that he willed it to become a woman and married her, but she went on pursuing mice—thus proving that "deflecting nature is absurd." Here Chagall has left La Fontaine's humor behind and injected his private world with its overtones of Edgar Allan Poe or a Russian ghost story. The result is a startling print.
Etching, 11⅝″ x 9½″, courtesy of the Museum of Modern Art, Larry Aldrich Fund.

227. CHAGALL, La Fontaine's *Fables*: The Swan and the Cook

A cook who has a lovely swan for a pet and a goose for food is about to kill the swan by mistake when she bursts into song. The moral: It's a good idea to speak up when you're in danger. In this entire series, Chagall's style is like that of a child drawing with chalk on the sidewalk. His is a fairy-tale world where there are no hard edges and composition seems accidental.

Etching, 11⅞″ x 15¼″, courtesy of the Museum of Modern Art, Larry Aldrich Fund.

228. CHAGALL, La Fontaine's *Fables*: The Lion and the Hunter

This fable tells of a hunter who, while furiously pursuing his lost dog, encounters a lion and cries for help. La Fontaine is saying that the test of valor lies in a man's behavior when faced with real danger—"some who sang bass, sing tenor." As usual, Chagall here makes a mockery of the formal art of etching and draws as if he were discovering a new world. Etching, 11⅞" x 15", courtesy of the Museum of Modern Art, Larry Aldrich Fund.

329

229. CHAGALL, Jacob Blessing the Children of Joseph

Compare this print to one by Dürer and see why artists have had to change their styles through the ages. Dürer's great line and bold drawing have been repeatedly copied by lesser artists. To get fresh impact from a familiar subject, the modern creator must experiment with new lines—here they are broken, misty, moody—and invent in his own time as Dürer did in his.

Etching, 11⅟₁₆″ x 9¾₁₆″, courtesy of the Museum of Modern Art, Larry Aldrich Fund.

230.   CHAGALL, The Bible: Jacob's Dream

Here the artist is like William Blake, whose ideas run ahead of his content. The law of gravity is mocked, and the angels in their homemade wings have yet to solo.

Etching, 13⅛″ x 17¼″, courtesy of the Museum of Modern Art, gift of Mr. and Mrs. Bernard J. Reis.

231. CHAGALL, The Bible: Solomon Proclaimed King

Innocence is the key to the artist's work. Here is none of the grand vulgarity of Paul Gustave Doré or the lush Hollywood-style treatment of Biblical subjects. Chagall sees with a fresh eye.

Etching, 13⅛" x 17¼", courtesy of the Museum of Modern Art, gift of Mr. and Mrs. Bernard J. Reis.

232. CHAGALL, The Rainbow

Chagall is unique among modern artists in capturing visions that seem to have come directly from those who first beheld them. If the Old Testament figure in the right-hand corner could have drawn his experience, this is what he might have put down.

Etching, 13⅛″ x 17¼″, courtesy of the Museum of Modern Art, gift of Mr. and Mrs. Bernard J. Reis.

ABOUT THE AUTHOR

STEPHEN LONGSTREET *is a painter and writer, whose family have for several generations been collectors of art. He had his first exhibition of pencil drawings at the age of four and a water-color show at eight. After graduation from the New York School of Fine and Applied Art, he spent the last half of the 1920s in Paris, Rome and London, studying painting. There he came to know such artists as Utrillo and Suzanne Valadon (whose story he told in* Man of Montmartre*); Chagall, Matisse and Picasso (the heroes of his novel,* The Burning Man*); and such notables of the period as Gertrude and Leo Stein, James Joyce, Elliot Paul and Ernest Hemingway.*

In the 1930s he returned to America to become an artist for The New Yorker *and a critic. Traveling to many parts of the world in a search for old and new art forms, he wrote two books about his experiences:* Last Man Around the World *and* The World Revisited.

His writings on art and artists are many; among them are Geisha, *a study of the lives of the great Japanese woodcut artists;* The Lion at Morning, *a novel about the American art world;* The Real Jazz Old and New *and* Encyclopédie du Jazz, *both of which contain his own paintings and drawings of jazz musicians together with text. In addition, he has published two best-selling novels outside the art field,* The Pedlocks *and* The Beach House. *He hopes to complete in the near future a large project long in work, "The Artist as the Historian of Society."*

An ardent collector and historian of prints and other graphic art, Mr. Longstreet is a trustee of the Los Angeles Art Association and of International World Arts. He has taught and lectured on the arts at many colleges, and is art critic for the Western newspapers of the Readers' Syndicate. His own paintings have been exhibited in major museums in the United States and abroad, and a major exhibition of his work is taking place in the fall of 1961 on the West Coast, where Mr. Longstreet now lives.